IRELAND

AN ILLUSTRATED YEARBOOK

1994

IVEAGH MARKETS MDCCCCVI

IRELAND

AN ILLUSTRATED YEARBOOK
1994

Illustration • Cathy Henderson

Text • W. H. Crawford

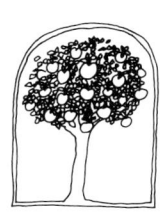

Appletree Press

First published by The Appletree Press Ltd, 19-21 Alfred Street, Belfast BT2 8DL. Illustrations © Cathy Henderson, 1993. Text © W. H. Crawford, 1993. Printed in the EC. All rights reserved. No part of this publication may be reproduced or transmitted in any form or by any means, electronic or mechanical, photocopying, recording or in any information or retrieval system, without prior permission in writing from the publishers.

Endpapers (front): The Lammas Fair, Ballycastle, Co. Antrim
(back): Fair Day, Maghera, Co. Derry

ISBN 0 86281 433 2

List of Illustrations

Mullingar Market-House, Mullingar, Co. Westmeath	*week* 1
Fair Day, Carrickmacross, Co. Monaghan	2
Corporation Flower Market, Dublin	3
Fair Day, Maghera, Co. Derry	4
Iveagh Market, Dublin	5
Clonbur, Co. Galway	6
Coal Quay Market, Cork	7
Aughnacloy, Co. Tyrone	8
Dundalk, Co. Louth	9
Dublin Horse Fair, Smithfield, Dublin	10
Bird Market, Off Bride Street, Dublin	11
Market Cross, Clones, Co. Monaghan	12
Navan, Co. Meath	13
Cattle Mart, Listowel, Co. Kerry	14
Coal Quay Market, Cornmarket Street, Cork	15
Fair Day, Dingle, Co. Kerry	16
Book Barrow Fair, Mansion House, Dublin	17
St George's Market, Belfast	18
Hiring Fair, The Diamond, Derry City	19
English Market, Cork	20
Fair Day, Belleek, Co. Fermanagh	21
Ballinasloe Horse Fair, Ballinasloe, Co. Galway	22
Glendalough, Co. Wicklow	23
Moore Street Market, Moore Street, Dublin	24
Clothes Market, Belfast	25
Sheep Auction, Maam Cross, Co. Galway	26
Dublin Horse Fair, Smithfield, Dublin	27
Spieler, Henry Street, Dublin	28
Ballinasloe Horse Fair, Ballinasloe, Co. Galway	29
Market-House, Newtownards, Co. Down	30

Thomas Street, Dublin	*week* 31
Blackberry Fair, Rathmines, Dublin	32
Puck Fair, Killorglin, Co. Kerry	33
Puck Fair, Killorglin, Co. Kerry	34
Donnybrook, Co. Dublin	35
The Lammas Fair, Ballycastle, Co. Antrim	36
Cumberland Street Market, Dublin	37
Former Butter Exchange, Cork	38
Mother Redcap's Market, Dublin	39
Vegetable Market, Belfast	40
Ballygawley, Co. Tyrone	41
Camden Street Market, Dublin	42
Fair Day, Longford, Co. Longford	43
Ardara, Co. Donegal	44
English Market, Cork	45
Fair Day, Dingle, Co. Kerry	46
High Street, Portadown, Co. Armagh	47
Corporation Fish Market, Dublin	48
South City Markets, Dublin	49
St George's Market, Belfast	50
Corporation Fruit and Vegetable Market, Dublin	51
Ballinasloe Horse Fair, Ballinasloe, Co. Galway	52
Iveagh Market, Dublin	53

Contributors

Cathy Henderson

Cathy Henderson attended Methodist College Belfast and subsequently spent a year working in Paris before studying at the National College of Art and Design in Dublin. Apart from a few months working in New York, she has remained in Dublin working on a wide variety of design and illustration commissions. In 1992 she completed an MA at the National College of Art and Design and in July of the same year had her first exhibition of prints and drawings.

W. H. Crawford

W. H. Crawford was introduced to the major sources for the study of the economic and social history of Ulster when he ran the education programme at the Public Record Office of Northern Ireland. In 1980 he became Keeper of Material Culture at the Ulster Folk and Transport Museum, retiring in 1993 to become the Development Officer for the Federation of Ulster Local Studies. His most recent publication is *The Hand-Loom Weavers in the Ulster Linen Industry*.

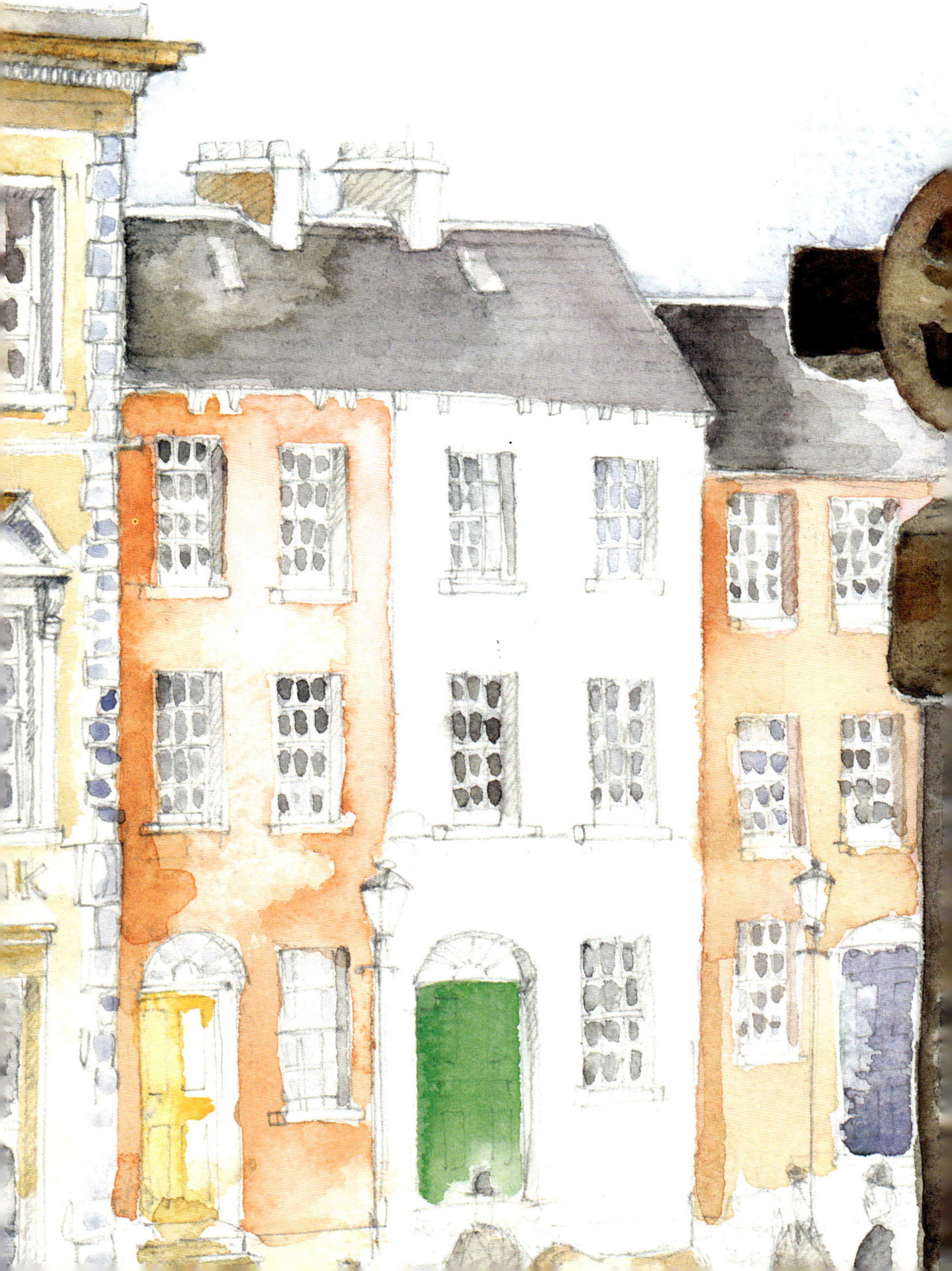

Introduction

The richness of Irish life in the past was reflected in the character of its fairs and markets. On these occasions folk flocked to the towns from the surrounding countryside to join in the excitement and the fun of buying and selling, drinking and fighting, singing and dancing, and meeting friends. These gatherings marked the high points of the year for countryfolk and they generated ballads and legends about the characters and exploits of those who frequented them. Their success indicated an economy where money was becoming more plentiful and clever men were trying to obtain their share of it.

In the past, lawyers could distinguish between a *market* and a *fair*. A market was intended to maintain the town in which it was held, by providing the townspeople every week with a regular supply of food in return for goods and services. Of course, not every town was able, in the long run, to support a weekly market: many smaller places had to be content with a fortnightly or even a monthly market. A fair, in contrast, was held on a few occasions each year to dispose of the surplus produce of a district, whether it was livestock or agricultural produce. In time, however, the number of fairs annually increased, at first to quarterly or seasonal fairs and later in many places to monthly cattle fairs held on 'the fair day'. By the nineteenth century it was common practice for markets to be held on a fixed day in the week and to have one of these days designated as the fair day in the month, for example the fourth Wednesday.

Since medieval times the right to hold markets and fairs had been granted in the form of parchment documents, known as patents, to individuals or corporations by English monarchs. In return for the right to charge tolls and customs to dealers, the owners of the fairs or their agents were required to provide standard weights and measures, maintain law and order, and to settle disputes at a Court of

Piepowder (from the French *pied poudré*, dusty feet), which lasted throughout the duration of the festival. In corporate towns, market juries were selected annually by the townspeople to examine the produce and maintain standards, while in estate towns the landlords' agents maintained manor courts which appointed supervisors of the markets.

It was essential for owners to organise and regulate their markets and fairs in order to maintain their reputation for honest dealing in a peaceful atmosphere. They had their work cut out for them because until the nineteenth century they could not rely on a peace-keeping force to maintain law and order. Faction-fighting was a common occurrence: wherever bad blood existed between rival groups, challenges were issued and drink was a powerful stimulant. In the late eighteenth century landlords used their local companies of volunteers to suppress disturbances, but it was the Royal Irish Constabulary in the following century who set a personal example by arresting notorious disturbers of the peace. The sheer scale of the great fairs was amazing. Ballinasloe in the late eighteenth century was reckoned to be one of the greatest fairs in all Europe: cattle were collected from Connacht and north Leinster to be fattened in Munster first for the Cork victualling trade and later for export to Britain.

The fairs especially bred a race of dealing men throughout the country. A clever man who had 'an eye for a beast' did not require capital to start up in the business. During his childhood he would have picked up a wide range of skills that enabled him to work the market. Without money he would have acted as a 'tangler' or a 'blocker', meeting farmers on the way to market and getting involved in deals before selling out his rights to a genuine dealer. With enough cash at his disposal he could exploit the anxiety of farmers to sell their beasts in an open market, especially when rents to their landlords were due. If he was really well-informed about the movement of prices, he could afford to buy in the sure knowledge that a profit was guaranteed. The most powerful of all dealers were the shippers who exported the animals to Britain, and they could afford to employ many men and treat an army of hangers-on.

More exciting than the cattle fairs were the great horse fairs because with horses there was always an element of danger as well as plenty of deceit. Indeed, it was said that there was 'no more deceitful race of men than jockeys in their sale of horseflesh'. Their ambition was to sell an unsound horse for a sound price. In preparation for the fair all its bad points had to be disguised or explained away as positive virtues. The animals were doctored with drugs and potions to make them spirited while the older animals were bishoped to make them appear much younger than they were. It was claimed that the worst horses were sold after dark. The heyday of the horse fairs preceded the First World War, for many of the British cavalry regiments were mounted on Irish horses while continental buyers frequented the great fairs at Moy in Tyrone, Ballybay in Monaghan, and Ballinasloe.

Other animals such as sheep and goats, donkeys, and occasionally pigs were sold in the fairs. But what could one think at the sight of rows of young girls and boys waiting to be hired every May and November? They looked as defenceless as the animals. They had trekked from their homes in the poorest districts in search of someone who would give them work, their keep, and a few pounds to take home at the end of their hire. They might be lucky enough to be taken in by a kind family, but there were many more poor farmers scraping a living with little to spare for a child.

The character of the fairs and markets was always changing. As long as the landlords ruled society they ensured that their towns submitted to the monthly invasion by the farmers and tidied up the aftermath. In the early nineteenth century the balance swung in favour of the townspeople and some of the new town commissioners began to move the cattle off the streets and restrict their sale to fair greens. Because the majority of these new town commissioners were shopkeepers and tradesmen they were not sympathetic to those who sold goods in the public market. Even after a mass movement in the east of Ireland in the 1820s and 1830s compelled many owners of fairs and markets to abandon charging customs and tolls on the dealers, town commissioners managed to reimpose similar charges for the use of market stalls and the use of the town weighbridge. Banks and merchants became the major source of credit, the constabulary enforced law and order, and railways transported the cattle to the seaports. These were the factors that underpinned the golden age of traditional Irish fairs which provided a good living for many dealers during the first half of the twentieth century.

By then other changes were taking place. Foreign competition in the British market compelled both governments, North and South, to improve marketing standards: registration of breeding sires, veterinary examination, grading of produce, and the selling of animals by weight. The coming of radio enabled farmers to learn more quickly about comparative market prices while the availability of motor transport extended their market range. Over the years more farmers were attracted to the sale rings organised in cities by auctioneers, and after the Second World War these marts spread to the provincial towns.

It was the same with the markets for agricultural produce. Shippers of potatoes and rye-grass seed, for example, had been buying at their own stores for many years because they had better facilities than the public markets and the farmers trusted that they would obtain a fair price. The creamery movement made a similar impact on sales of butter and milk. As a result, the weekly markets in towns declined, especially in competition with the shops which were importing a greater range of goods and selling them on more favourable terms. The market folk were forced to concentrate on cheap goods, often seconds or second-hand, on seasonal fruit and vegetables, and on dulse and yellow-man.

Market and fairs will continue to play a significant

role in our society because folk are still looking for bargains, but even more because they enjoy the fun of the fair, the element of the unexpected, the patter of the dealers and even the whole makeshift element. Concourses of people continue to attract musicians and ballad singers, showmen and gamblers. These lessons have not been lost on the managers of some of our modern supermarkets or on those who promote every sort of one-day show from craft fairs to jumble sales.

W. H. Crawford

IRELAND

AN ILLUSTRATED YEARBOOK
1994

MARKET HOUSE

Mí na Nollag-Eanáir ● Dezember-Januar ● Décembre-Janvier

1993-94 DECEMBER-JANUARY

Monday Luan Montag Lundi ● Week 1

27

Tuesday Máirt Dienstag Mardi

28

Wednesday Céadaoin Mittwoch Mercredi

29

Thursday Déardaoin Donnerstag Jeudi

30

Friday Aoine Freitag Vendredi

31

Saturday Satharn Samstag Samedi
New Year's Day Lá Coille

1

Sunday Domhnach Sonntag Dimanche

2

MULLINGAR MARKET-HOUSE
**Mullingar,
Co. Westmeath**

This fine market-house was built in the late eighteenth century when Mullingar, the county town for Westmeath, was owned by the Earl of Granard. Mullingar's wool, horse, and cattle fairs were considered to be inferior only to those of Ballinasloe, while its Thursday markets did great business in grain, butter and provisions.

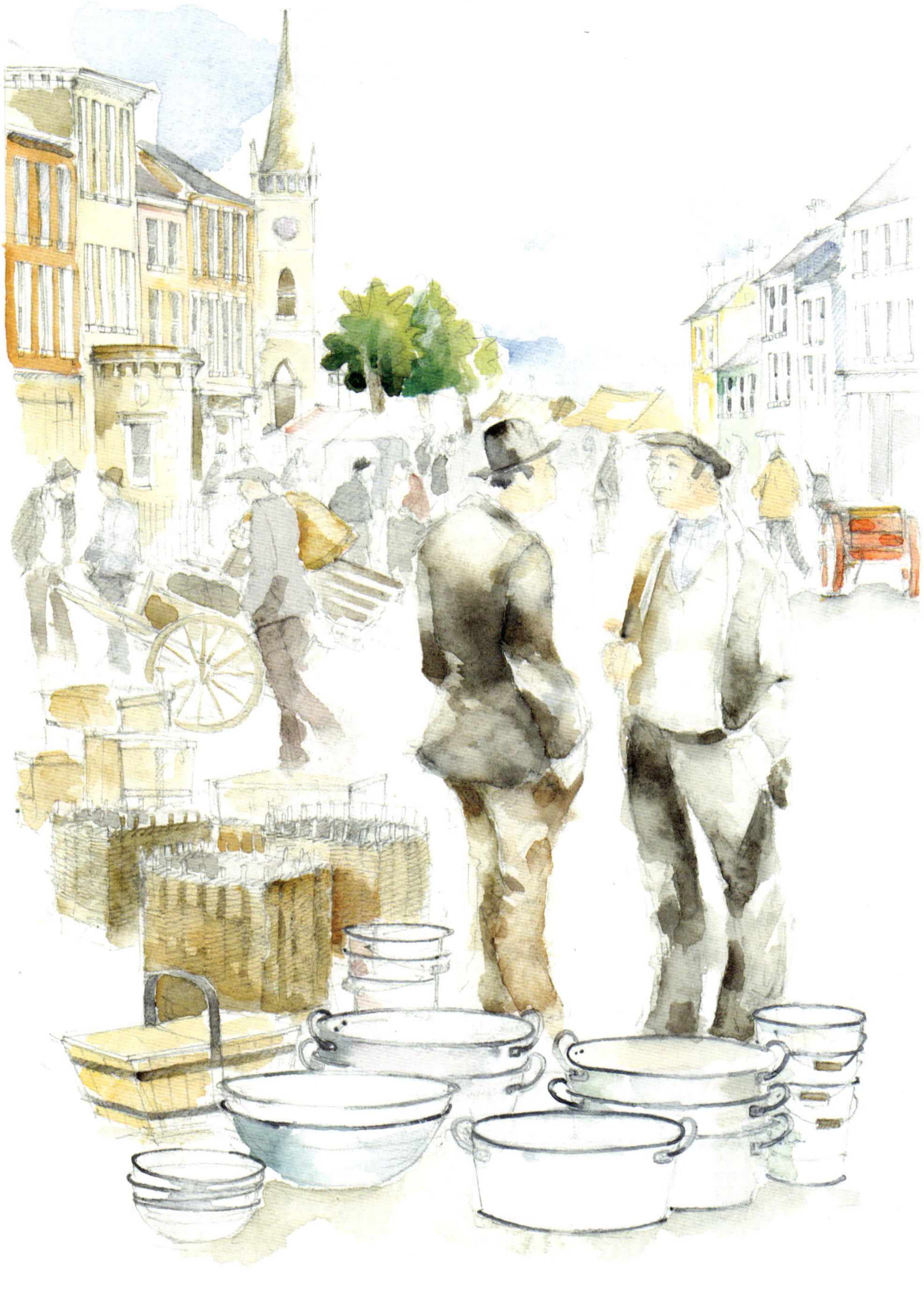

1994 Eanáir • Januar • Janvier
JANUARY

Monday Luan Montag Lundi • Week 2

3

Tuesday Máirt Dienstag Mardi

4

Wednesday Céadaoin Mittwoch Mercredi

5

Thursday Déardaoin Donnerstag Jeudi

6

Friday Aoine Freitag Vendredi

7

Saturday Satharn Samstag Samedi

8

Sunday Domhnach Sonntag Dimanche

9

**FAIR DAY
Carrickmacross,
Co. Monaghan**

By the 1890s new materials were appearing in the market. The term 'galvanised iron' denoted iron dipped in zinc, and it was used for making cheap baths and buckets that would stand up to rust, as well as for corrugated iron. Enamelled buckets and basins were also in demand because they were hygienic. The baskets, however, were made locally.

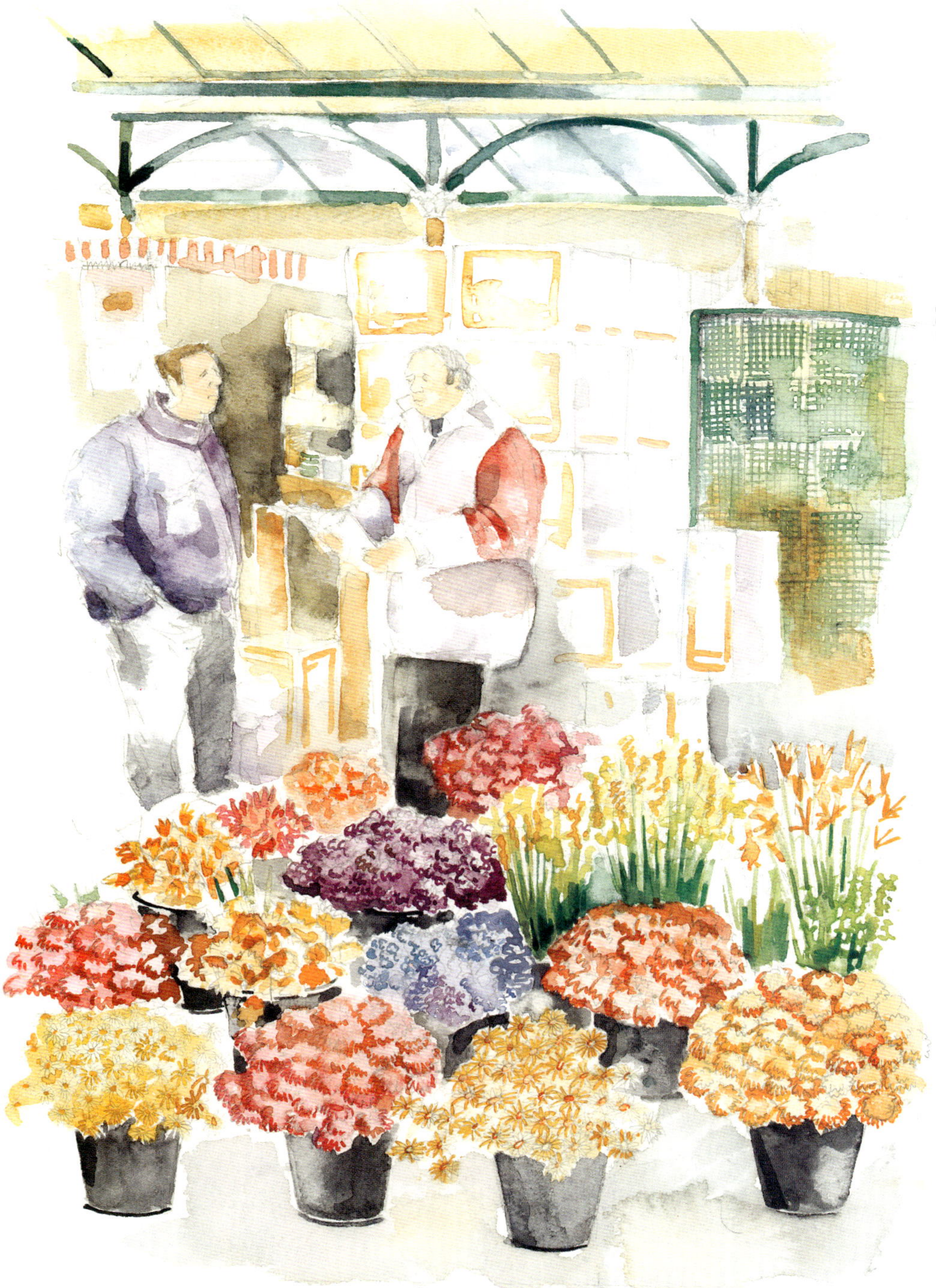

Eanáir • Januar • Janvier

1994　　　　　　　　　　JANUARY

Monday Luan Montag Lundi • Week 3

10

Tuesday Máirt Dienstag Mardi

11

Wednesday Céadaoin Mittwoch Mercredi

12

Thursday Déardaoin Donnerstag Jeudi

13

Friday Aoine Freitag Vendredi

14

Saturday Satharn Samstag Samedi

15

Sunday Domhnach Sonntag Dimanche

16

**CORPORATION FLOWER MARKET
Dublin**

Flower-giving is among the most popular and best appreciated of social conventions: as tokens of respect for the deceased; as expressions of thanks to hostesses and of affection for friends and loved ones; as cheering gifts to housebound folk; and as decorations at weddings and ceremonies. Nowadays the range of choice is remarkable when so many varieties can be imported from foreign countries.

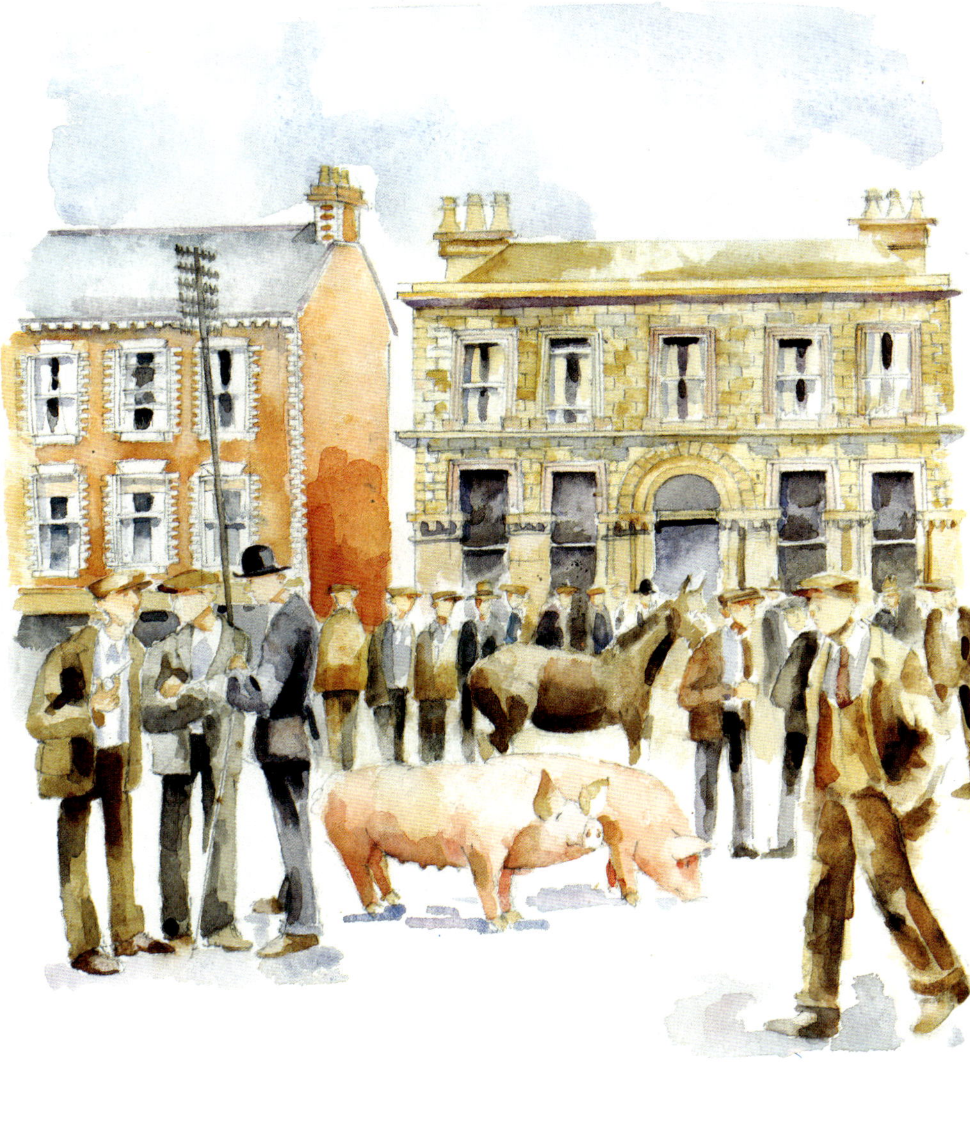

Eanáir • Januar • Janvier

1994 JANUARY

Monday Luan Montag Lundi • Week 4

17

Tuesday Máirt Dienstag Mardi

18

Wednesday Céadaoin Mittwoch Mercredi

19

Thursday Déardaoin Donnerstag Jeudi

20

Friday Aoine Freitag Vendredi

21

**FAIR DAY
Maghera, Co. Derry**

Pig production in Ulster was based mainly on a dead pork trade and pig slaughtering generally took place on the farm until the introduction of the pig marketing scheme in 1933. Breeding sows and litters of piglets were sold in the fairs. The large white Ulster pig has been replaced by leaner varieties.

Saturday Satharn Samstag Samedi

22

Sunday Domhnach Sonntag Dimanche

23

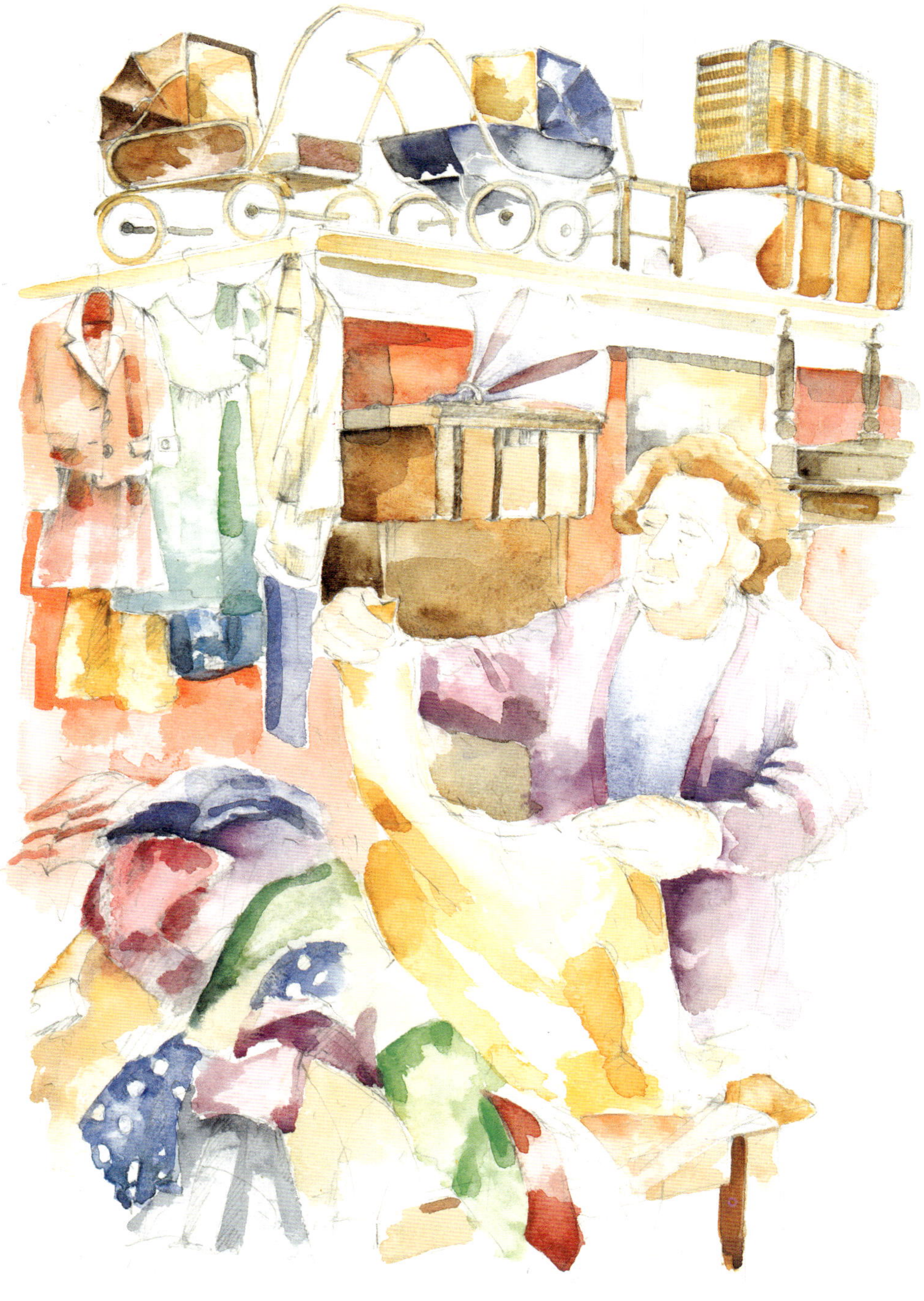

Eanáir • Januar • Janvier

1994 JANUARY

Monday Luan Montag Lundi • Week 5 — **24**

Tuesday Máirt Dienstag Mardi — **25**

Wednesday Céadaoin Mittwoch Mercredi — **26**

Thursday Déardaoin Donnerstag Jeudi — **27**

Friday Aoine Freitag Vendredi — **28**

Saturday Satharn Samstag Samedi — **29**

Sunday Domhnach Sonntag Dimanche — **30**

**IVEAGH MARKET
Dublin**

The Iveagh Markets, founded in 1906, is only a shadow of its former glory. Customers no longer flock to buy the second-hand clothes. 'Tuggers' went round the doors buying anything they considered saleable. Then the clothes were disinfected near the markets by the Corporation and washed in the laundry. They performed a valuable service for the local community.

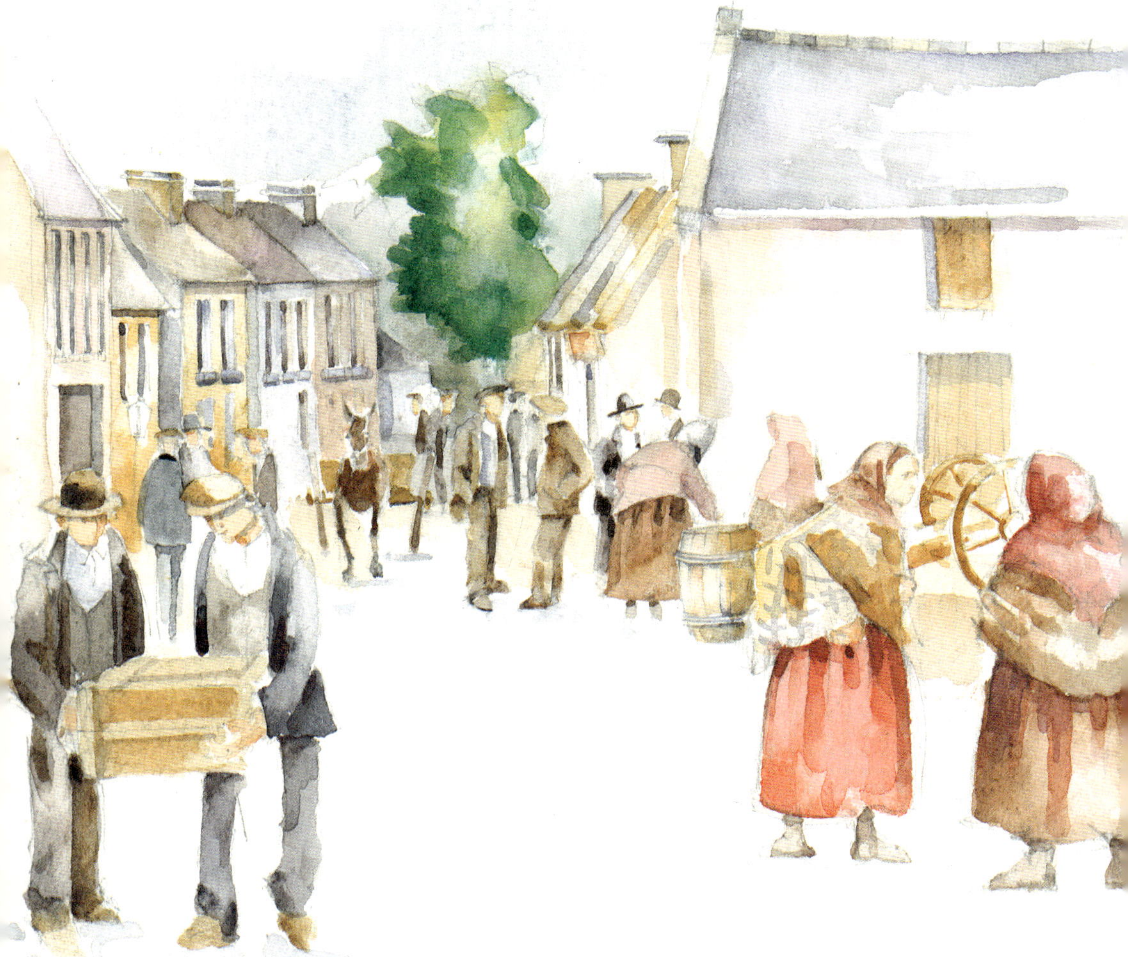

Eanáir-Feabhra • Januar-Februar • Janvier-Février

1994 JANUARY-FEBRUARY

Monday Luan Montag Lundi • Week 6

31

Tuesday Máirt Dienstag Mardi

1

Wednesday Céadaoin Mittwoch Mercredi

2

Thursday Déardaoin Donnerstag Jeudi

3

Friday Aoine Freitag Vendredi

4

Saturday Satharn Samstag Samedi

5

Sunday Domhnach Sonntag Dimanche

6

CLONBUR
Co. Galway

Clonbur lies in the parish of Ross on the isthmus that separates Lough Mask from Lough Corrib, and just on the Galway side of the border with Mayo. It was typical of many of the small hamlets in this part of the world but unusual in that it possessed a Saturday market where great quantities of corn were sold. There were also four fairs on 1 February, 17 March, 1 July and 1 September for general farming stock.

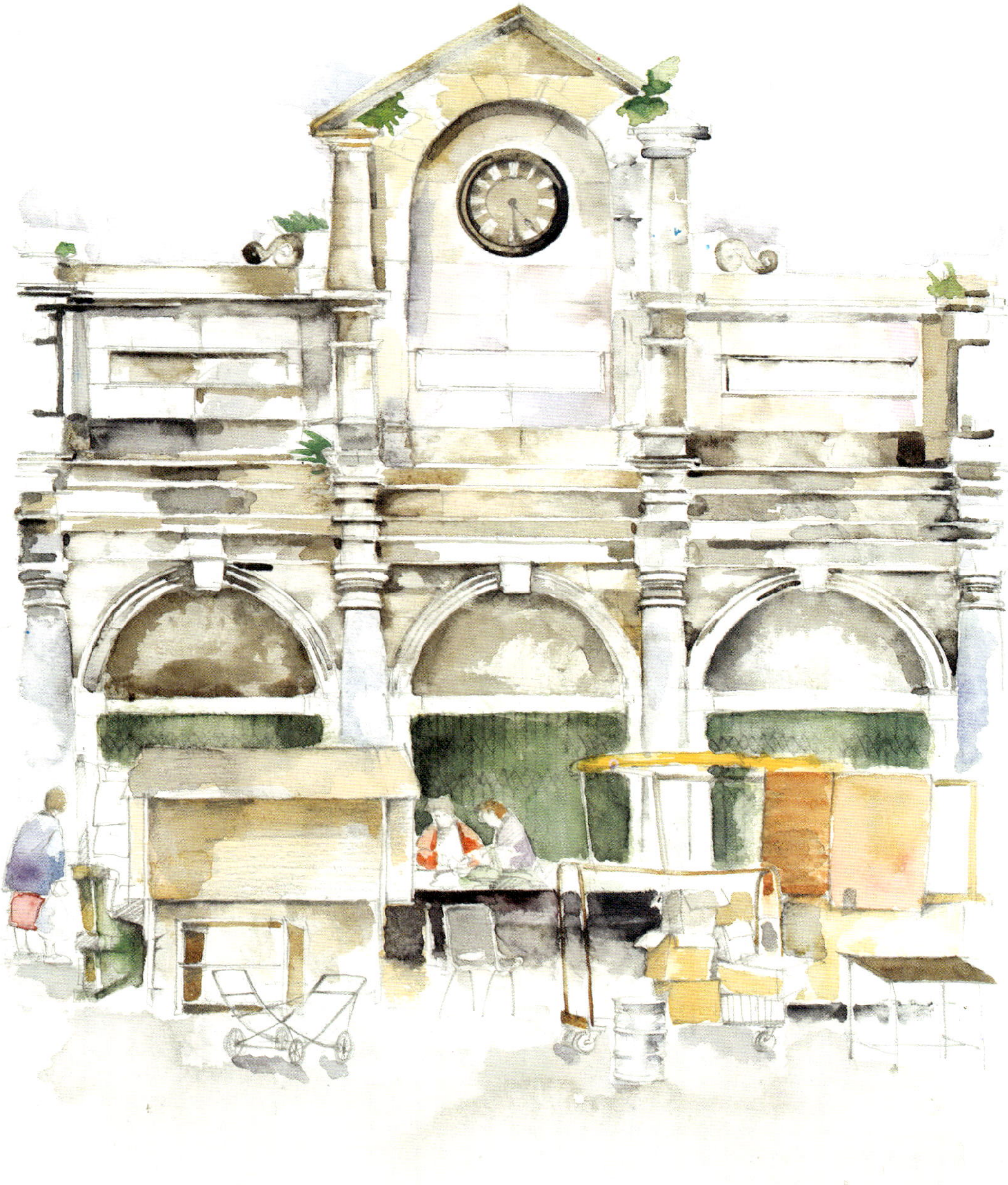

1994   Feabhra • Februar • Février
FEBRUARY

Monday Luan Montag Lundi • Week 7   **7**

Tuesday Máirt Dienstag Mardi   **8**

Wednesday Céadaoin Mittwoch Mercredi   **9**

Thursday Déardaoin Donnerstag Jeudi   **10**

Friday Aoine Freitag Vendredi   **11**

Saturday Satharn Samstag Samedi   **12**

Sunday Domhnach Sonntag Dimanche   **13**

**COAL QUAY MARKET
Cork**

In *The Ancient and Present State of the County and City of Cork*, published in 1760, Charles Smith commented: 'The new corn market-house is a large commodious edifice, erected on pillars of the Tuscan order, of hewn stone, in a place convenient for the carriage of corn, meal, etc. by water, but in so narrow a situation that it is almost hid.'

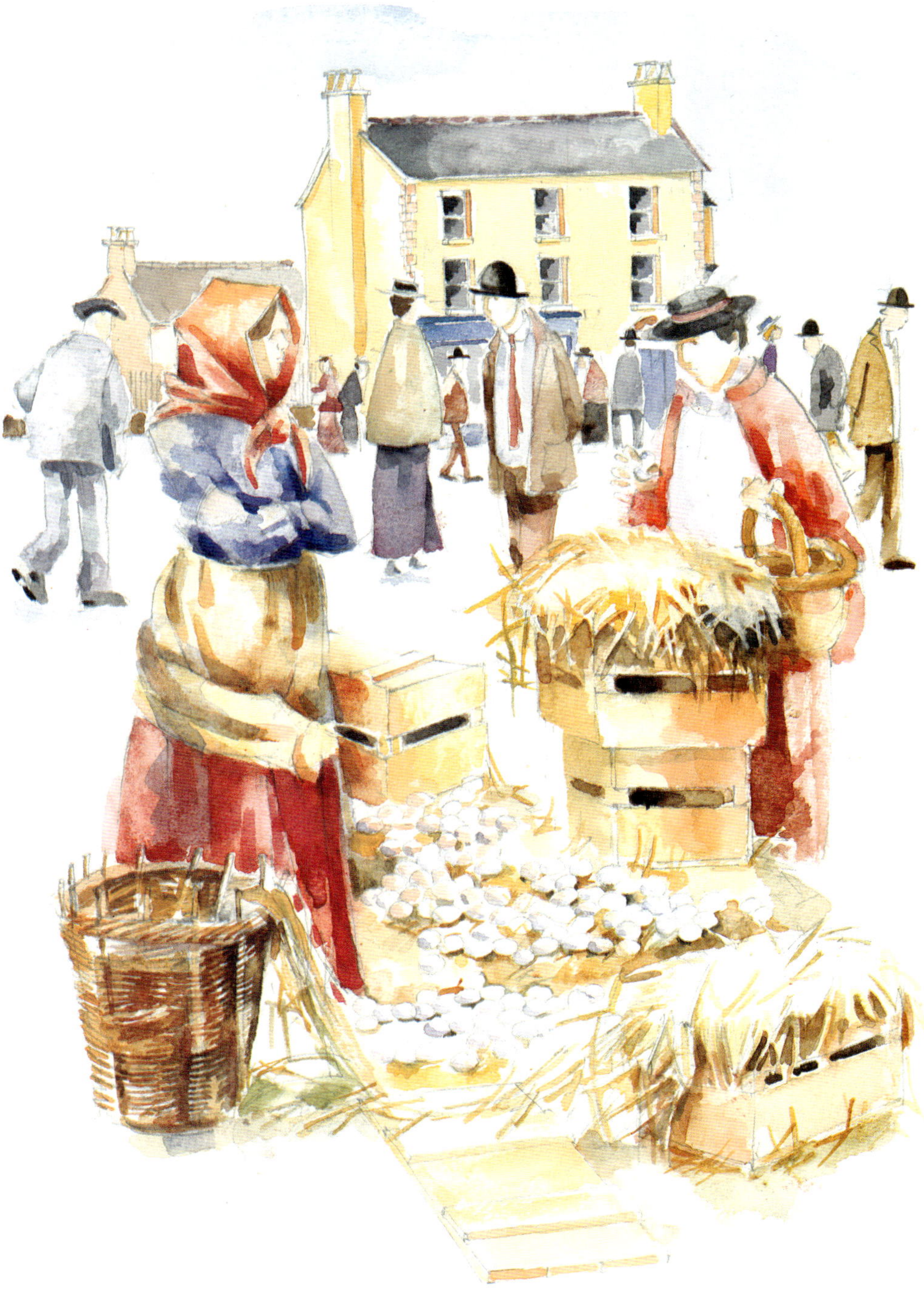

Feabhra • Februar • Février

1994　　　　　　　　　　　　　　　FEBRUARY

Monday Luan Montag Lundi • Week 8　　**14**

Tuesday Máirt Dienstag Mardi　　**15**

Wednesday Céadaoin Mittwoch Mercredi　　**16**

Thursday Déardaoin Donnerstag Jeudi　　**17**

Friday Aoine Freitag Vendredi　　**18**

Saturday Satharn Samstag Samedi　　**19**

Sunday Domhnach Sonntag Dimanche　　**20**

AUGHNACLOY
Co. Tyrone

On their way to market women used to bring eggs to sell for ready cash. In the mid nineteenth century the buyer used to make a large nest of straw on which to collect the eggs. Straw was also used for packing egg boxes for export until about 1910 when the Department introduced insulation moulded in soft cardboard.

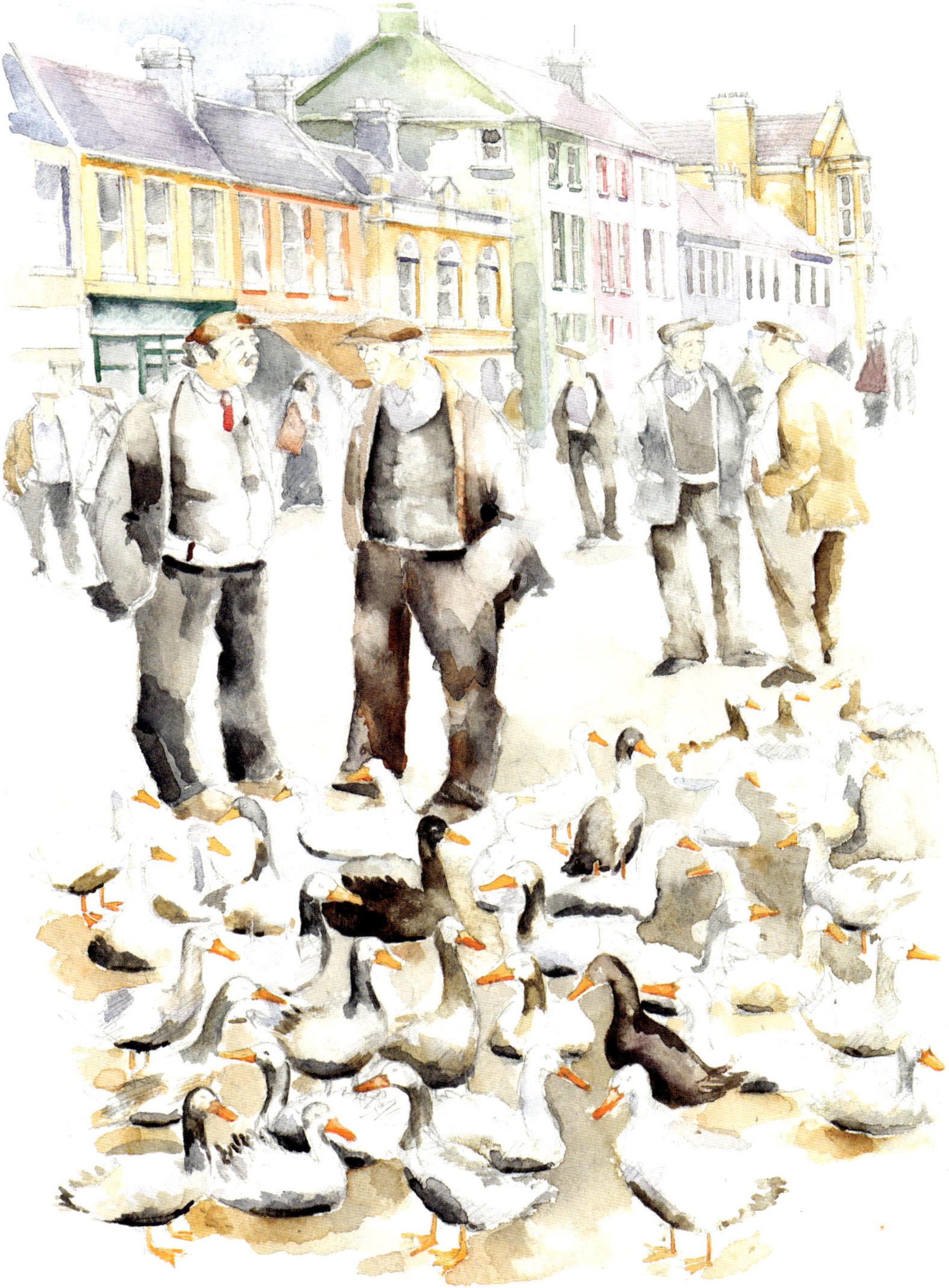

Feabhra • Februar • Février

1994　　　　　　　　　　　　　　FEBRUARY

Monday Luan Montag Lundi • Week 9　　　　**21**

Tuesday Máirt Dienstag Mardi　　　　**22**

Wednesday Céadaoin Mittwoch Mercredi　　　　**23**

Thursday Déardaoin Donnerstag Jeudi　　　　**24**

Friday Aoine Freitag Vendredi　　　　**25**

Saturday Satharn Samstag Samedi　　　　**26**

Sunday Domhnach Sonntag Dimanche　　　　**27**

DUNDALK
Co. Louth

The importance of poultry in the farming economy is easily overlooked. In 1900 it was estimated that the produce of twenty chickens equalled a cow in value. At that date Ireland had more than fifteen million hens, three million ducks, two million geese and one million turkeys.

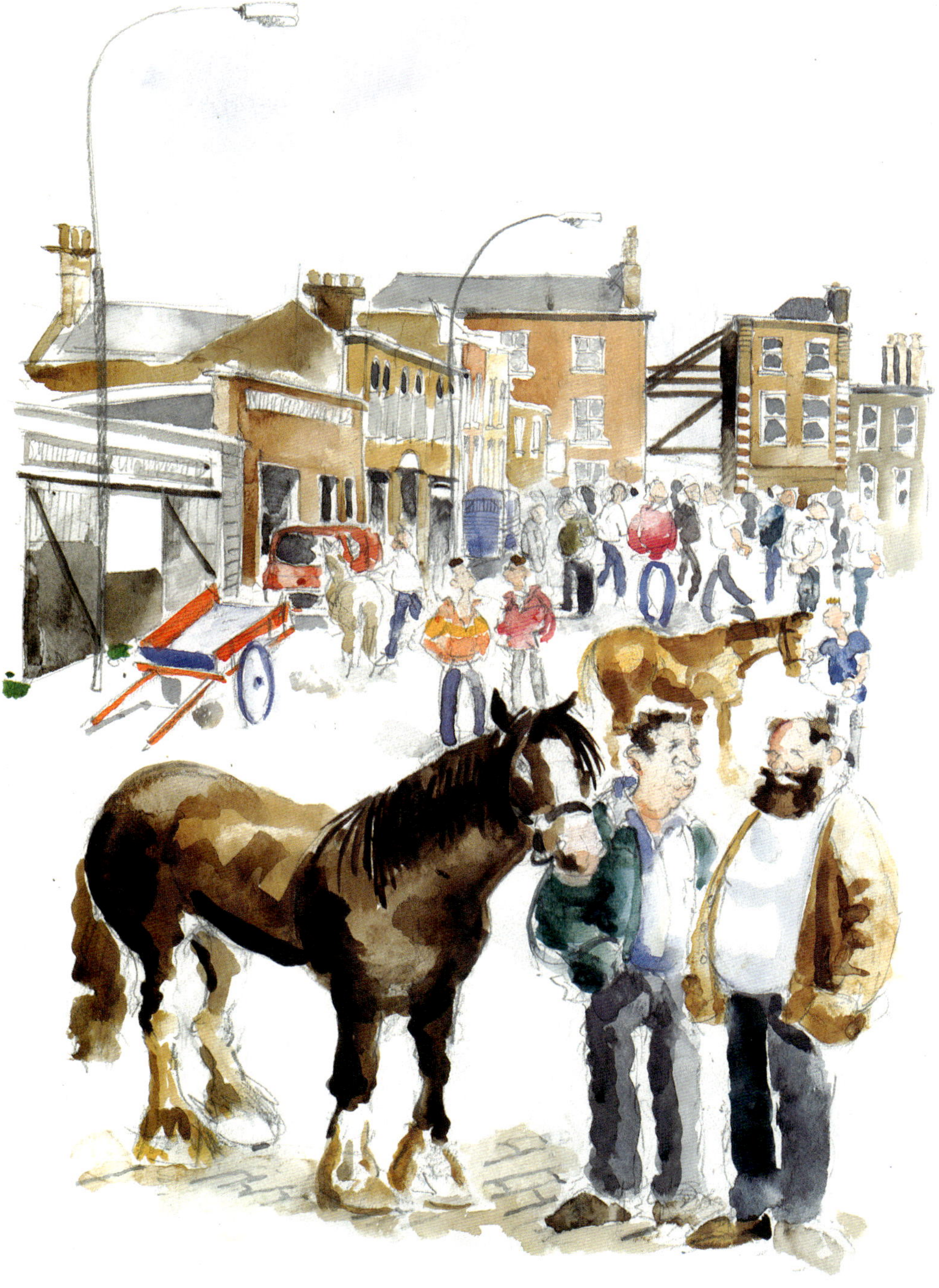

1994 FEBRUARY-MARCH

Feabhra-Márta • Februar-März • Février-Mars

Monday Luan Montag Lundi • Week 10 — **28**

Tuesday Máirt Dienstag Mardi — **1**

Wednesday Céadaoin Mittwoch Mercredi — **2**

Thursday Déardaoin Donnerstag Jeudi — **3**

Friday Aoine Freitag Vendredi — **4**

Saturday Satharn Samstag Samedi — **5**

Sunday Domhnach Sonntag Dimanche — **6**

DUBLIN HORSE FAIR
Smithfield, Dublin

On the first Sunday in each month a horse fair is still held at Smithfield in Dublin. It denotes the survival of a great tradition, for in the first half of the century no other European capital was more dependent on the horse. Although the famous dealers no longer tour the country fairs to purchase and organise the transport of great numbers of horses, they still appreciate a good horse.

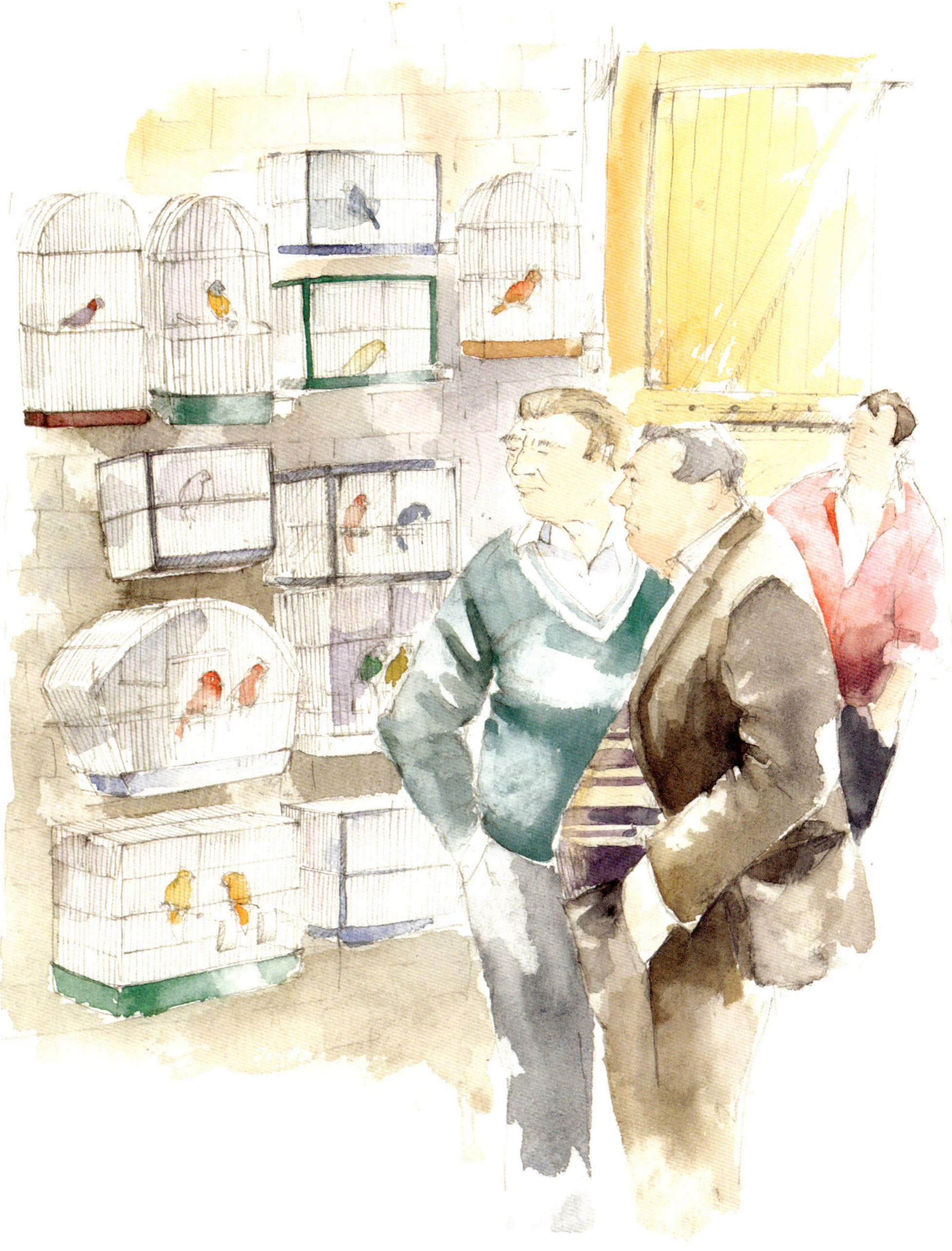

Márta • März • Mars

1994　　　　　　　　　　　MARCH

Monday Luan Montag Lundi • Week 11　　　　**7**

Tuesday Máirt Dienstag Mardi　　　　**8**

Wednesday Céadaoin Mittwoch Mercredi　　　　**9**

Thursday Déardaoin Donnerstag Jeudi　　　　**10**

Friday Aoine Freitag Vendredi　　　　**11**

Saturday Satharn Samstag Samedi　　　　**12**

Sunday Domhnach Sonntag Dimanche　　　　**13**

BIRD MARKET
Off Bride Street, Dublin

The Bird Market may have a history of more than three centuries, but it is still held on Sunday mornings in a small yard off Bride Street. The locals used to catch songbirds in the country around Dublin and at the bird market would sell them for a shilling or two to the folk who lived in the tenements. Cages hung outside the windows of many homes.

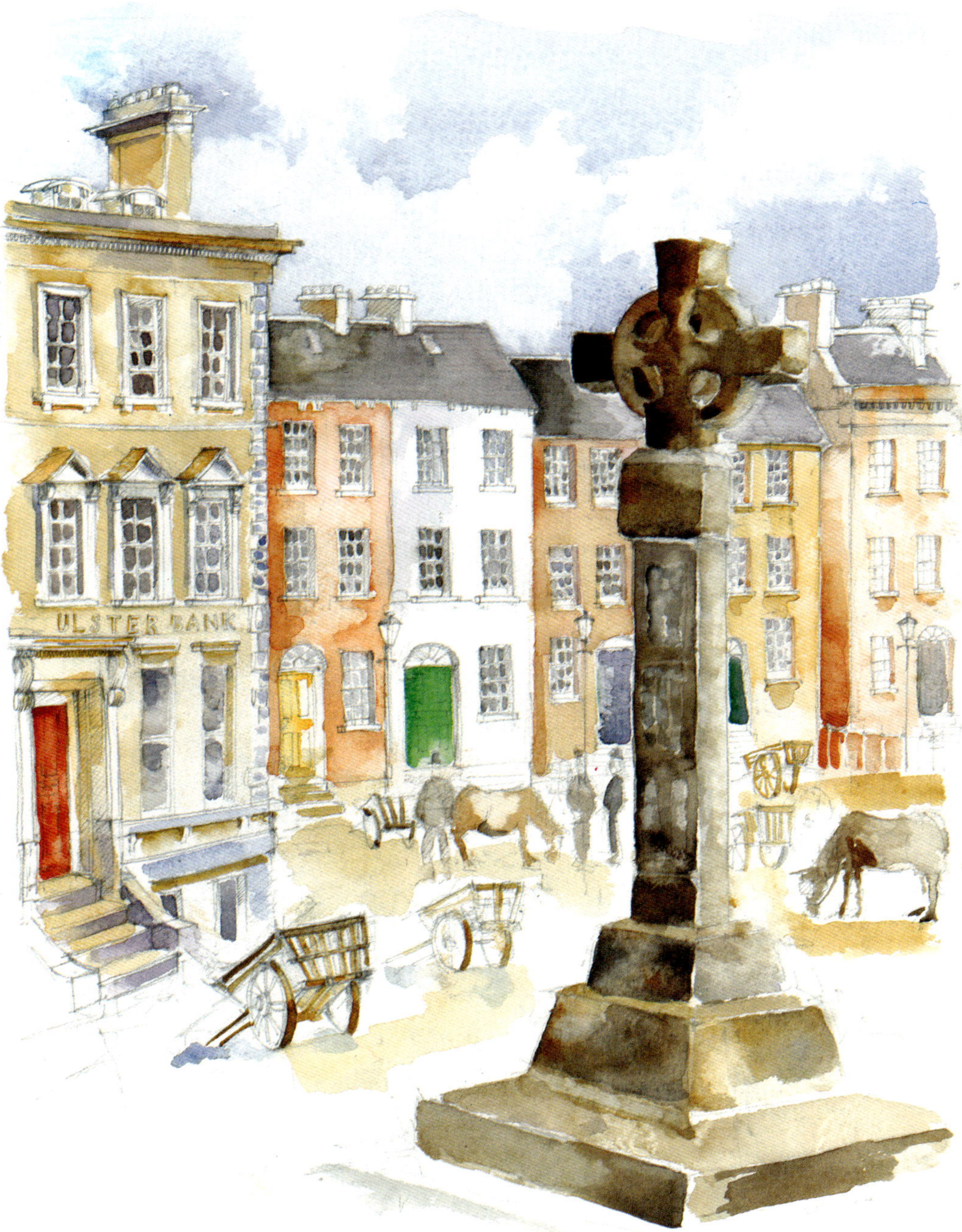
ULSTER BANK

Márta • März • Mars

1994 MARCH

Monday Luan Montag Lundi • Week 12

14

Tuesday Máirt Dienstag Mardi

15

Wednesday Céadaoin Mittwoch Mercredi

16

Thursday Déardaoin Donnerstag Jeudi
St Patrick's Day   Lá Fhéile Phádraig
Bank & public holiday

17

Friday Aoine Freitag Vendredi

18

Saturday Satharn Samstag Samedi

19

Sunday Domhnach Sonntag Dimanche

20

MARKET CROSS
Clones, Co. Monaghan

Market crosses were erected in many towns in medieval times to indicate the location of the market. This one in Clones, County Monaghan, appears on a map of 1590. It is composed of two separate pieces that once belonged to neighbouring monasteries. Many others have disappeared, the victims of old age, municipal vandalism or traffic accidents.

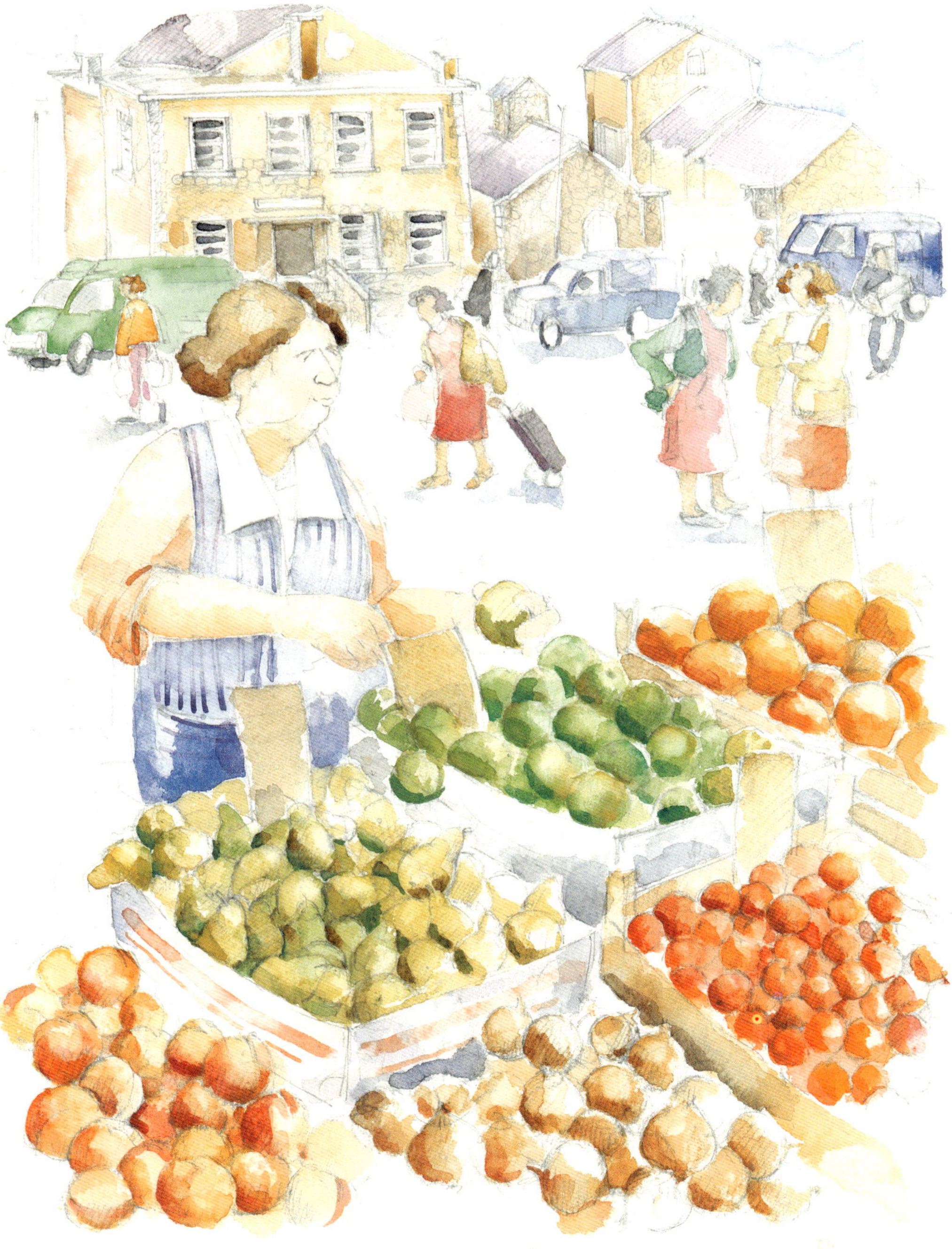

1994　　　　　　　　　　　Márta • März • Mars
MARCH

Monday Luan Montag Lundi • Week 13　　**21**

Tuesday Máirt Dienstag Mardi　　**22**

Wednesday Céadaoin Mittwoch Mercredi　　**23**

Thursday Déardaoin Donnerstag Jeudi　　**24**

Friday Aoine Freitag Vendredi　　**25**

Saturday Satharn Samstag Samedi　　**26**

Sunday Domhnach Sonntag Dimanche　　**27**

**NAVAN
Co. Meath**

In the years before the Great Famine, Navan's Wednesday market was well supplied with corn, pigs, coarse linens and frieze cloth, and there were four seasonal fairs for livestock. Nowadays the market has to concentrate more on fresh fruit and vegetables as well as the bargain trade. It was the growth of the service and retail sectors that have compensated for the declining importance of the fair.

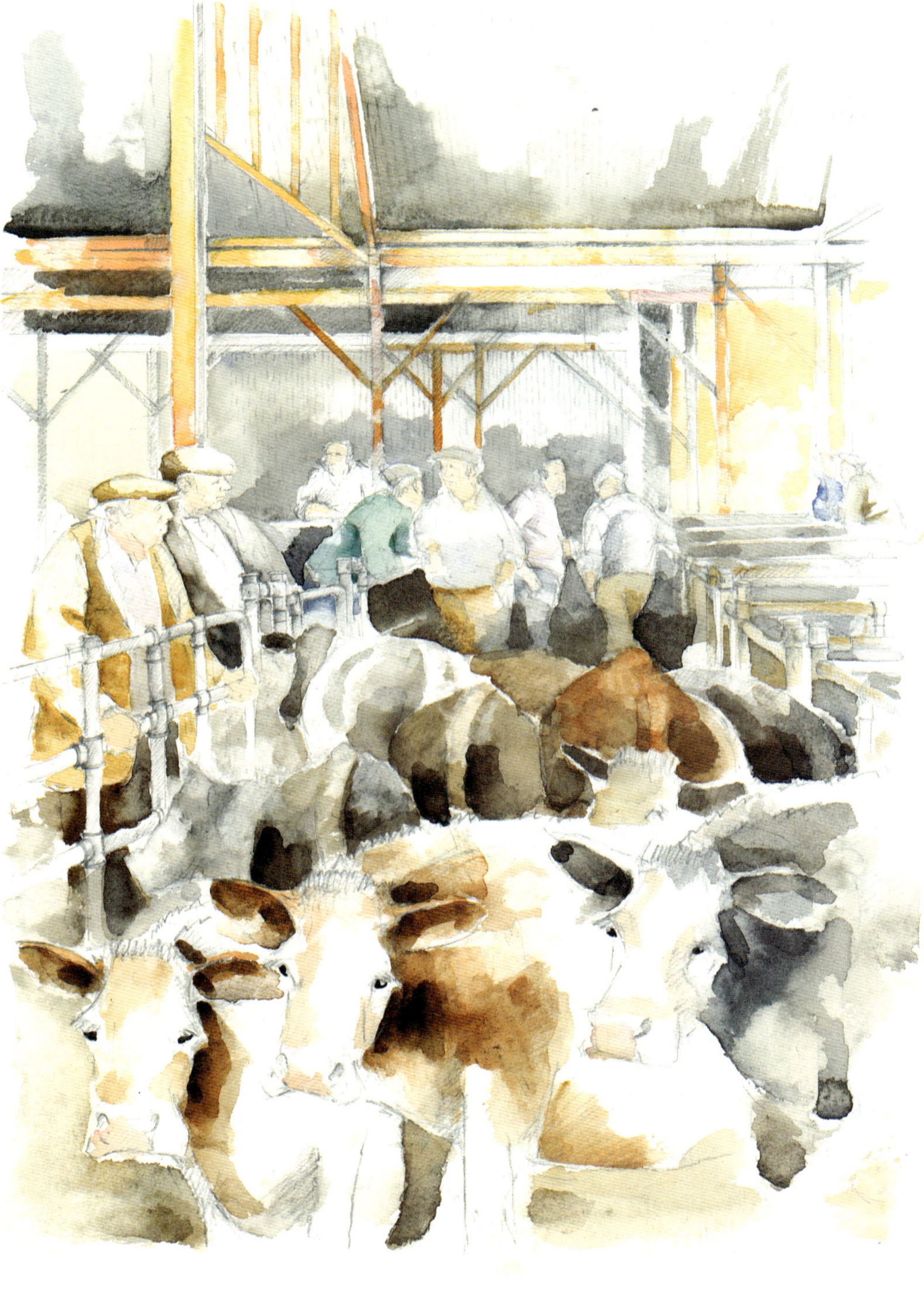

Márta-Aibreán • März-April • Mars-Avril

1994   MARCH-APRIL

Monday Luan Montag Lundi • Week 14   **28**

Tuesday Máirt Dienstag Mardi   **29**

Wednesday Céadaoin Mittwoch Mercredi   **30**

Thursday Déardaoin Donnerstag Jeudi   **31**

Friday Aoine Freitag Vendredi   **1**
Good Friday
Bank holiday

Saturday Satharn Samstag Samedi   **2**

Sunday Domhnach Sonntag Dimanche   **3**
Easter Sunday   Domhnach Cásca

CATTLE MART
Listowel, Co. Kerry

The last generation or two has seen the disappearance of the cattle fairs and the export of live cattle in face of the development of cattle marts throughout the country. Cattle are now inspected, graded, valued and sold to the meat plants who market the processed beef in European and world markets.

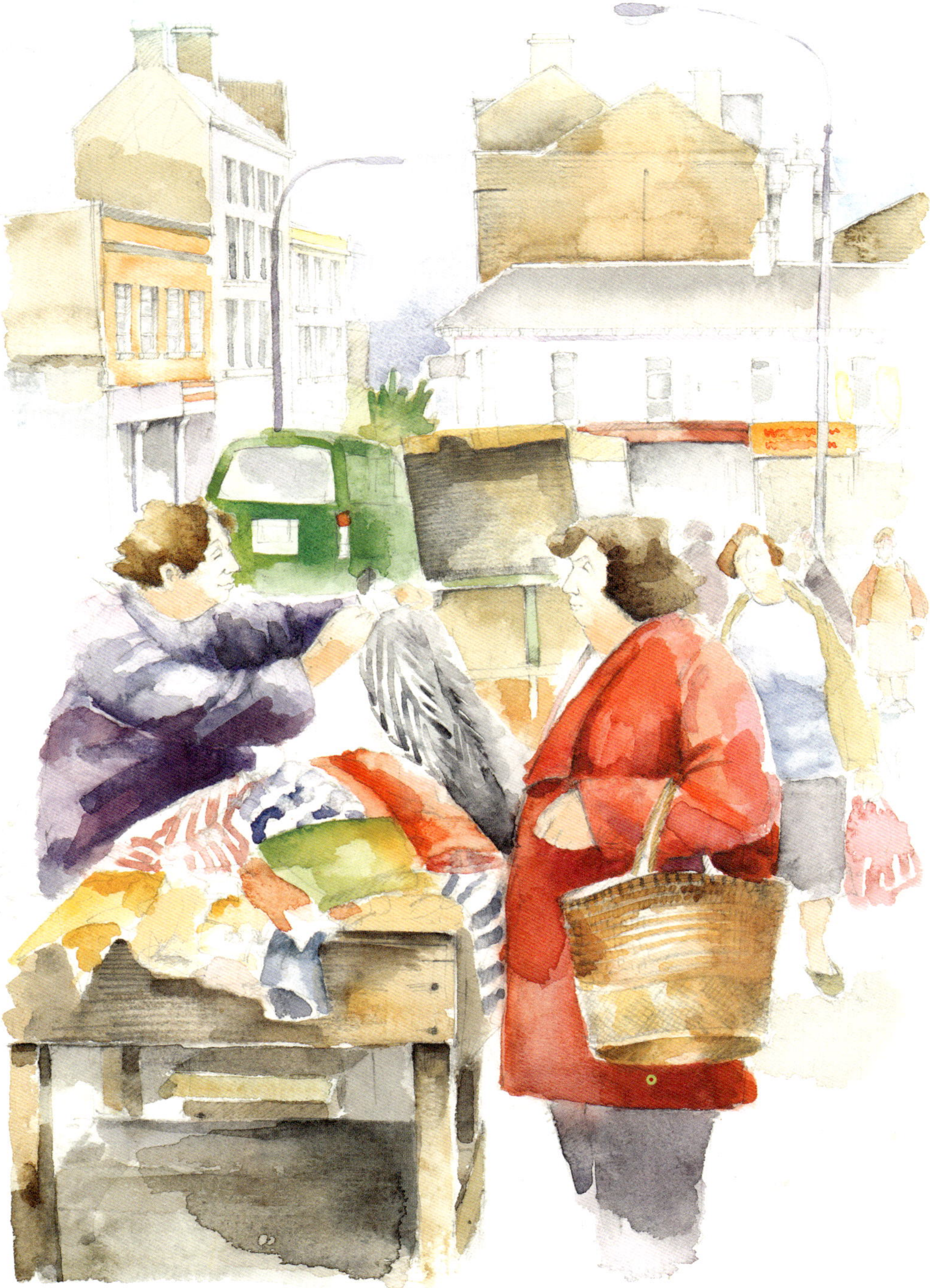

Aibreán ● April ● Avril

1994   APRIL

Monday Luan Montag Lundi ● Week 15
Easter Monday   Luan Cásca
Bank & public holiday

4

Tuesday Máirt Dienstag Mardi

5

Wednesday Céadaoin Mittwoch Mercredi

6

Thursday Déardaoin Donnerstag Jeudi

7

Friday Aoine Freitag Vendredi

8

Saturday Satharn Samstag Samedi

9

Sunday Domhnach Sonntag Dimanche

10

**COAL QUAY MARKET
Cornmarket Street, Cork**

The Coal Quay Market is not held on the Coal Quay in Cork but in the nearby Cornmarket Street. Like many open-air markets elsewhere, it tended to be dominated by the market women. An 1881 guide described this market as 'amusing enough to strangers, yet far too unfashionable for the respectable citizens to take much interest in'.

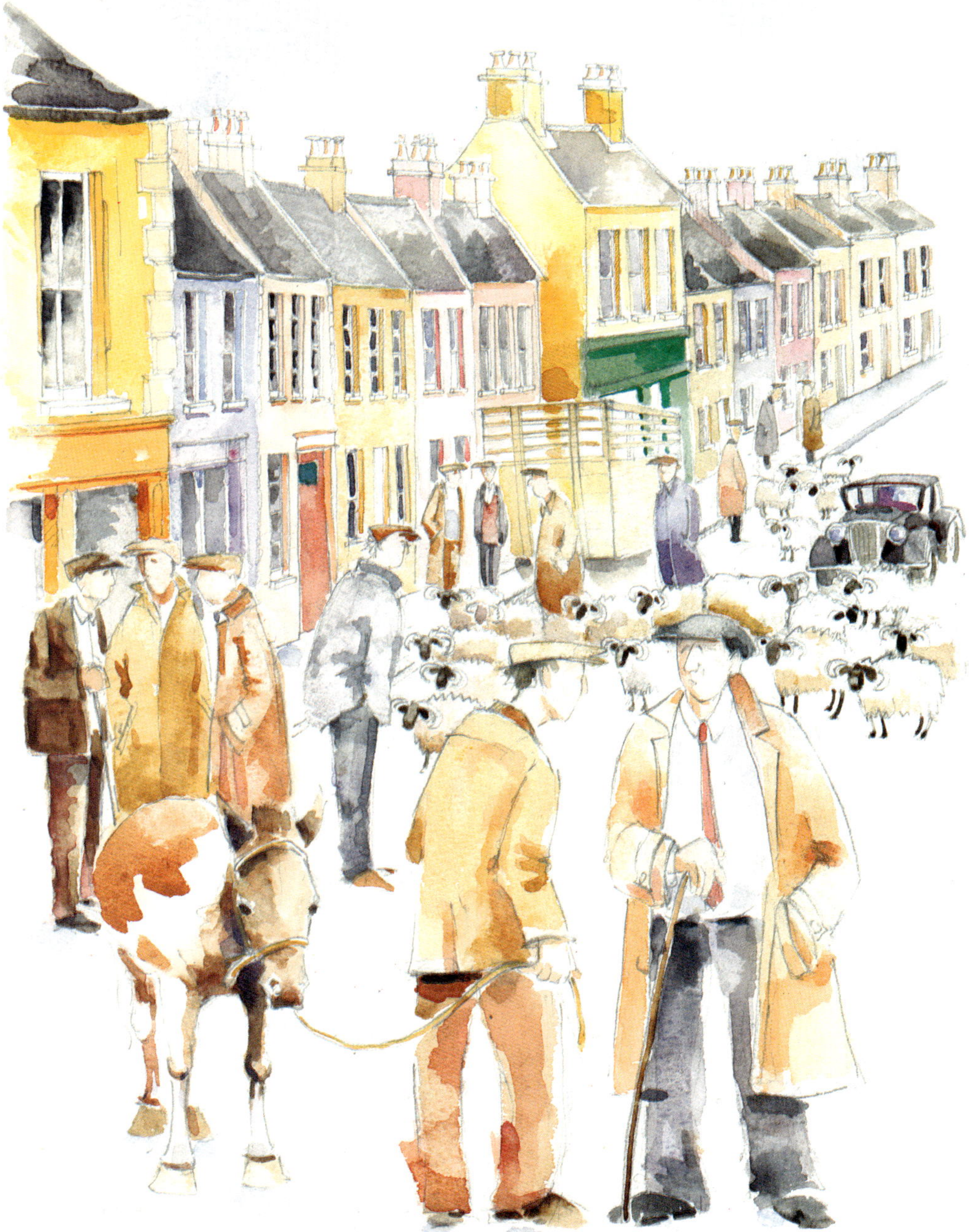

Aibreán • April • Avril

1994   APRIL

Monday Luan Montag Lundi • Week 16   **11**

Tuesday Máirt Dienstag Mardi   **12**

Wednesday Céadaoin Mittwoch Mercredi   **13**

Thursday Déardaoin Donnerstag Jeudi   **14**

Friday Aoine Freitag Vendredi   **15**

Saturday Satharn Samstag Samedi   **16**

Sunday Domhnach Sonntag Dimanche   **17**

**FAIR DAY
Dingle, Co. Kerry**

The 1960s marked the end of an era in Irish life. Between 1946 and 1961 the number of people engaged in agriculture in the South of Ireland fell by more than 218,000. Ireland had not yet enjoyed the benefits of membership of the European Economic Community.

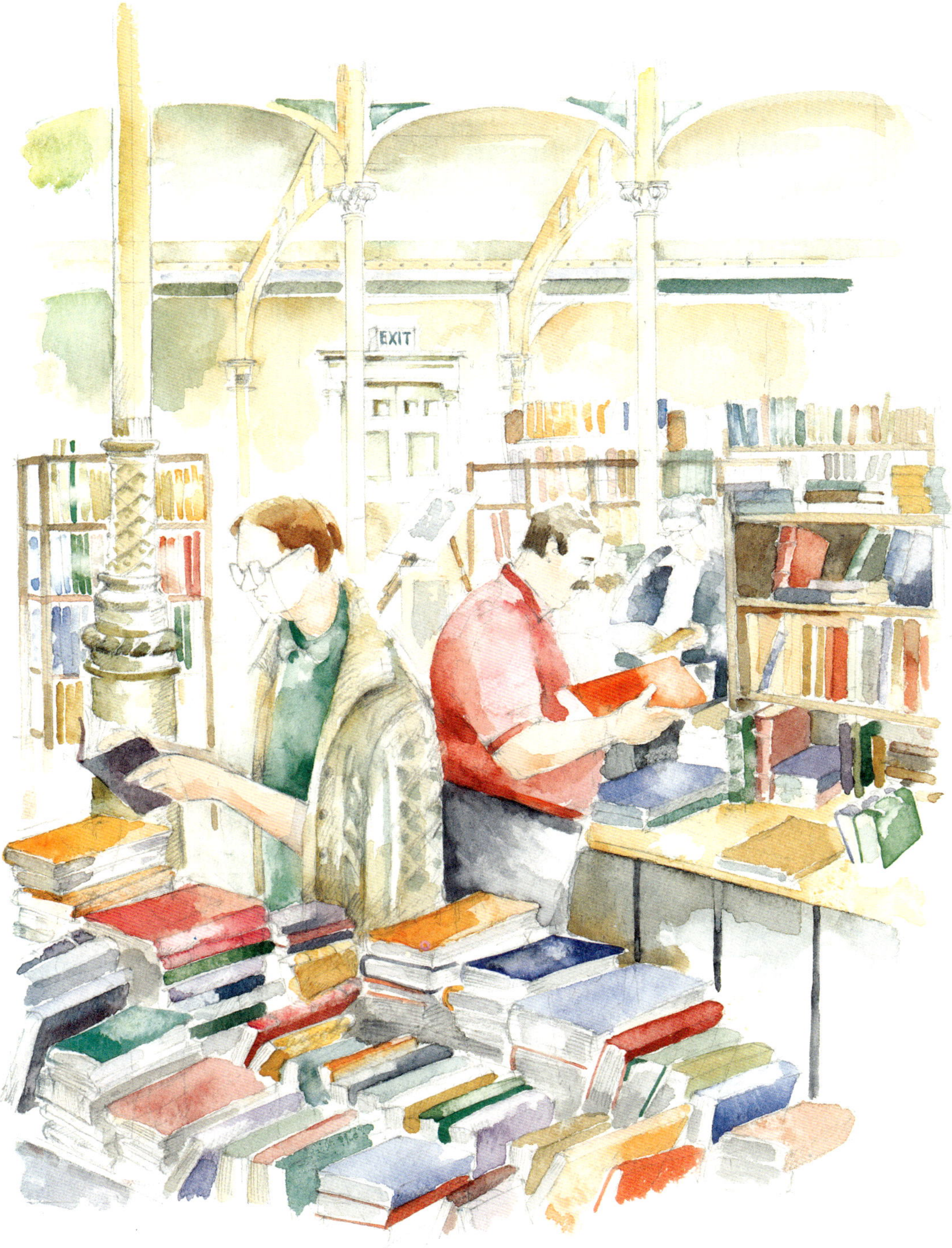
EXIT

Aibreán • April • Avril

1994   APRIL

Monday Luan Montag Lundi • Week 17   **18**

Tuesday Máirt Dienstag Mardi   **19**

Wednesday Céadaoin Mittwoch Mercredi   **20**

Thursday Déardaoin Donnerstag Jeudi   **21**

Friday Aoine Freitag Vendredi   **22**

Saturday Satharn Samstag Samedi   **23**

Sunday Domhnach Sonntag Dimanche   **24**

BOOK BARROW FAIR
Mansion House, Dublin

Most of us find great difficulty in passing a market for second-hand or remaindered books. After all, there is no compulsion to purchase and there is a good chance of finding a treasure or a volume that has eluded us over the years. And even if we come away without a purchase, the time has been well spent.

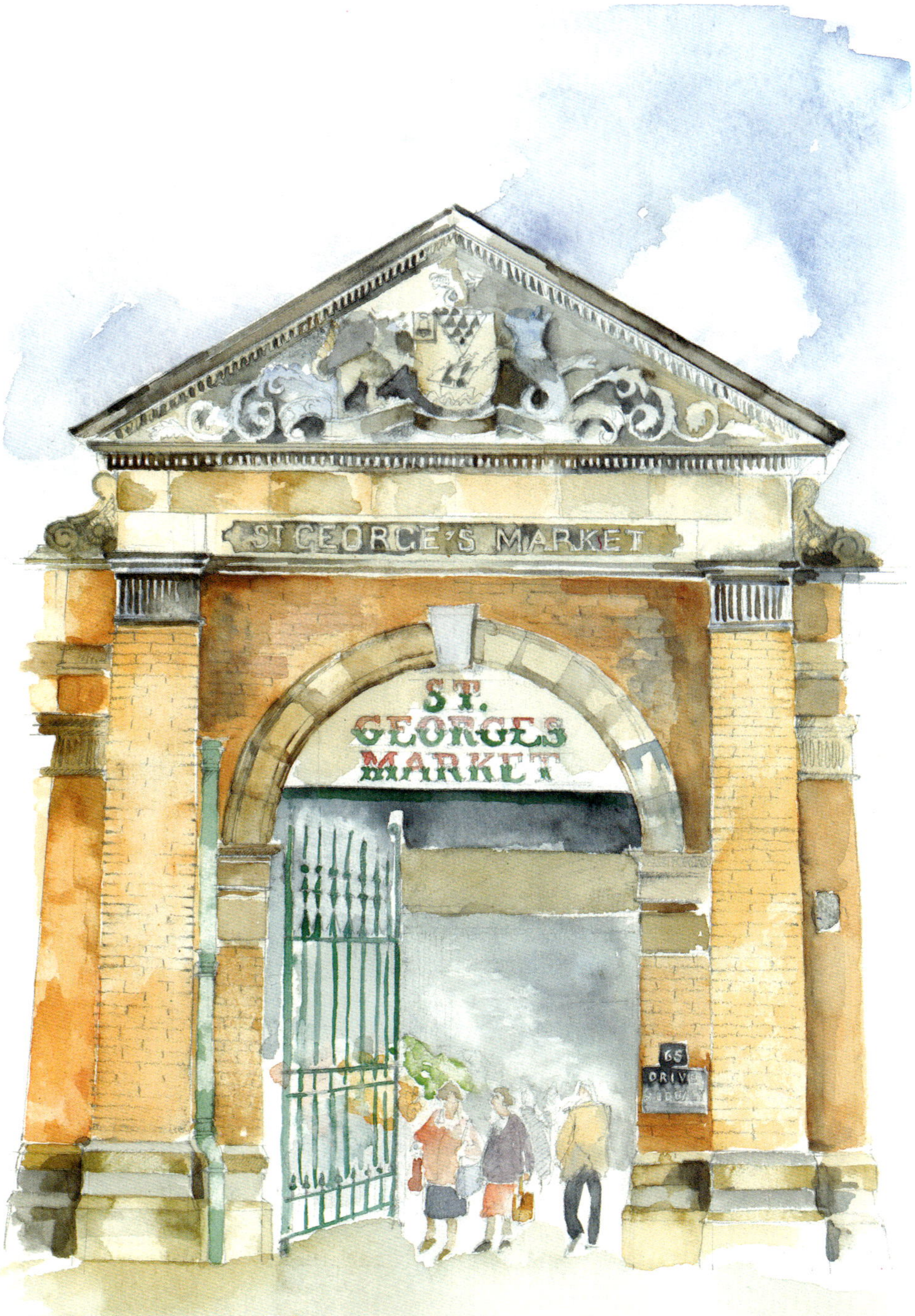
ST GEORGE'S MARKET
ST. GEORGES MARKET
65
DRIVE

Aibreán-Bealtaine • April-Mai • Avril-Mai

1994　　　　　　　　　APRIL-MAY

Monday Luan Montag Lundi • Week 18　　**25**

Tuesday Máirt Dienstag Mardi　　**26**

Wednesday Céadaoin Mittwoch Mercredi　　**27**

Thursday Déardaoin Donnerstag Jeudi　　**28**

Friday Aoine Freitag Vendredi　　**29**

Saturday Satharn Samstag Samedi　　**30**

Sunday Domhnach Sonntag Dimanche　　**1**

ST GEORGE'S MARKET
Belfast

St George's Market was built between 1890 and 1896 to a design by J. C. Bretland, the Belfast City Surveyor, to house the butter, egg and poultry markets. The fruit market also was fitted into it. Its compatriot the Fish Market, also by Bretland, has been demolished to make way for the new Laganbank project, but St George's is still a lively place on Friday mornings.

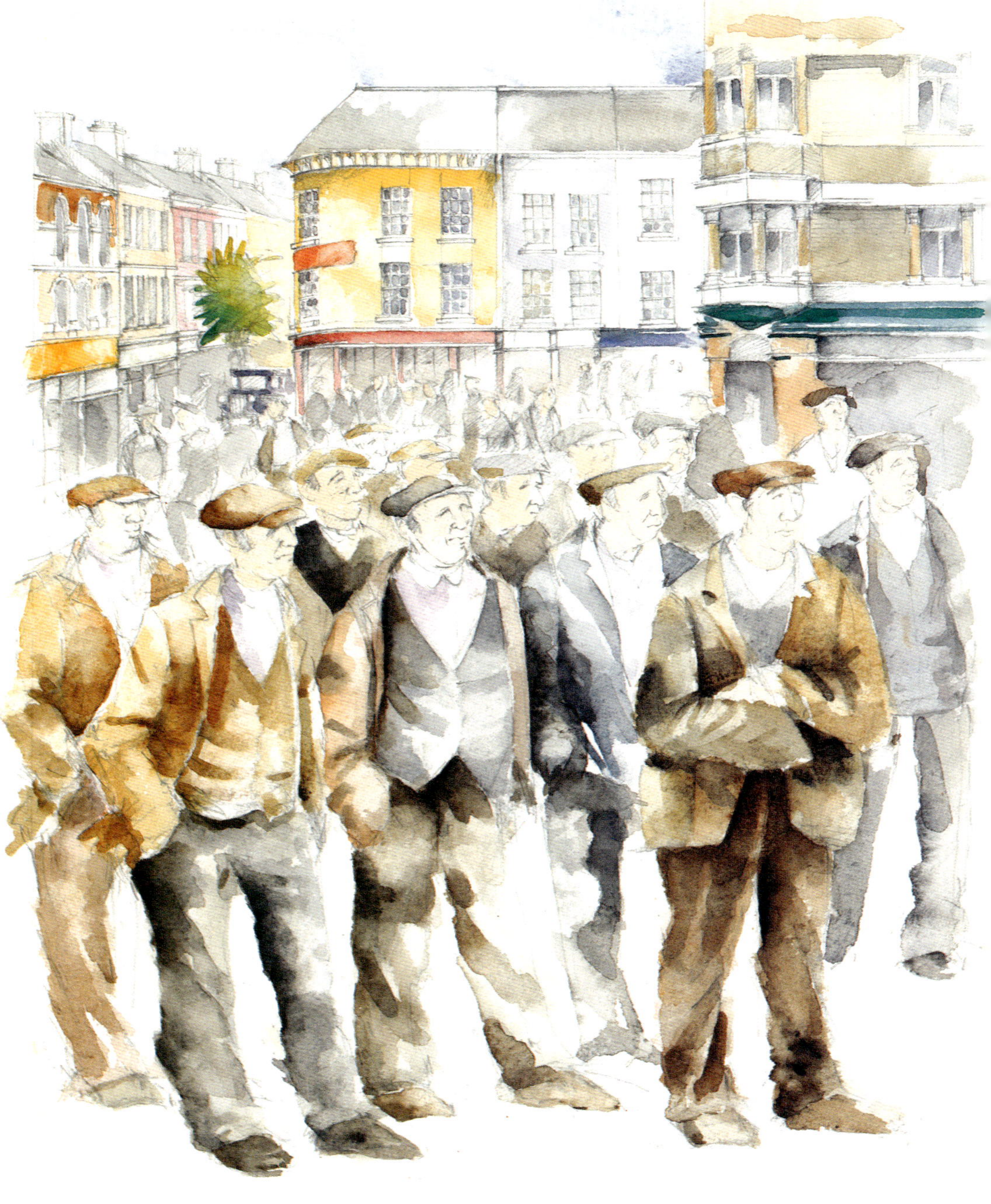

Bealtaine • Mai • Mai

1994   MAY

Monday Luan Montag Lundi • Week 19   **2**

Tuesday Máirt Dienstag Mardi   **3**

Wednesday Céadaoin Mittwoch Mercredi   **4**

Thursday Déardaoin Donnerstag Jeudi   **5**

Friday Aoine Freitag Vendredi   **6**

Saturday Satharn Samstag Samedi   **7**

Sunday Domhnach Sonntag Dimanche   **8**

HIRING FAIR
The Diamond, Derry City

From the late eighteenth century until the Second World War Derry was the gateway for many Donegal and Tyrone people seeking work. Youngsters trekked to the hiring fairs at Strabane, Letterkenny and Derry to obtain a place on the larger farms of the Laggan and north Londonderry. When they were older they headed for Scotland or even further.

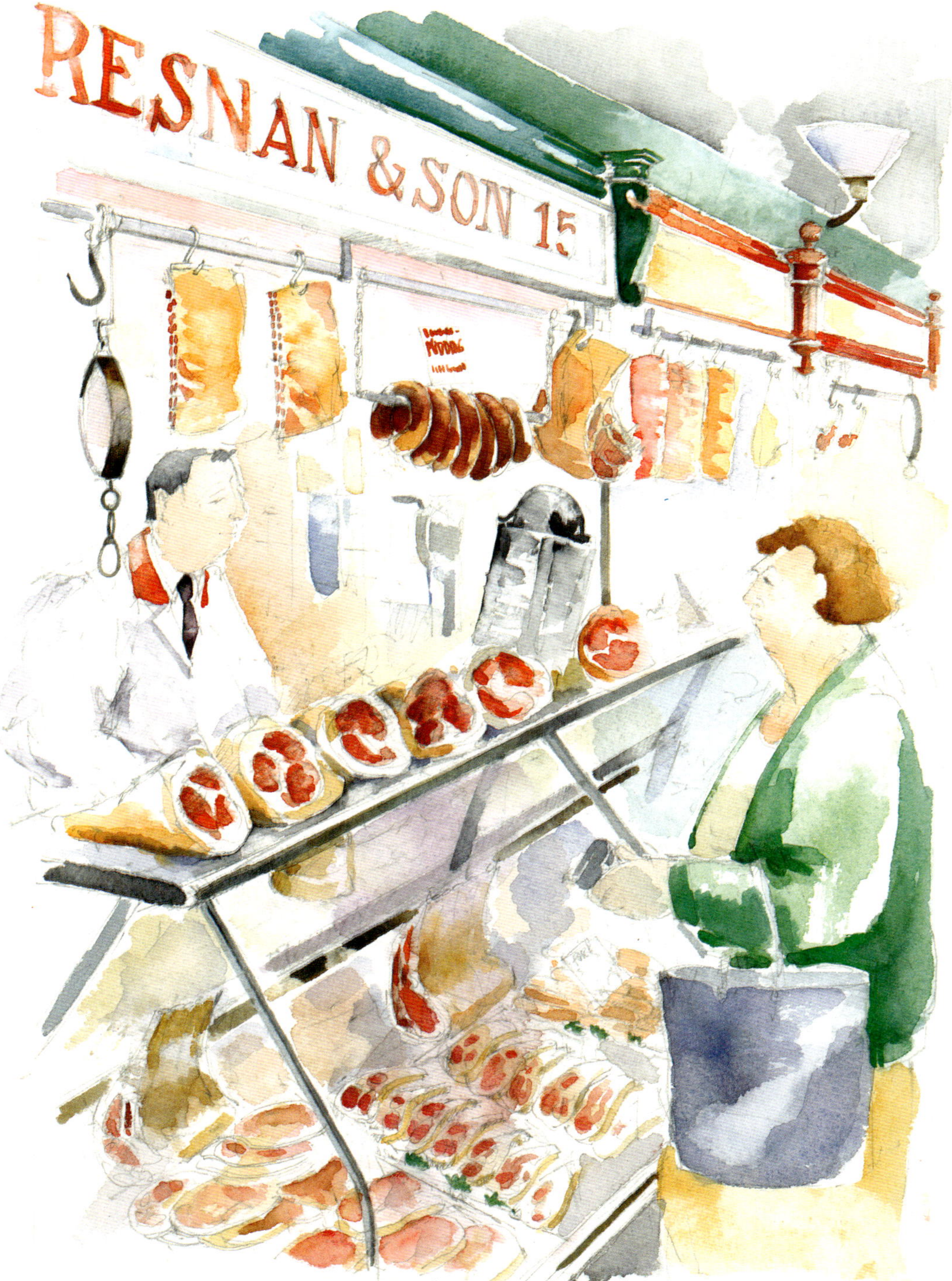
RESNAN & SON 15

Bealtaine • Mai • Mai

1994 MAY

Monday Luan Montag Lundi • Week 20

9

Tuesday Máirt Dienstag Mardi

10

Wednesday Céadaoin Mittwoch Mercredi

11

Thursday Déardaoin Donnerstag Jeudi

12

Friday Aoine Freitag Vendredi

13

Saturday Satharn Samstag Samedi

14

Sunday Domhnach Sonntag Dimanche

15

**ENGLISH MARKET
Cork**

Cork was once described as 'the shambles of Ireland' when the term shambles was used to describe a butcher's slaughter house. In the later eighteenth century it was estimated that every season 100,000 cattle were slaughtered. It was said of its pork butchers that they could use every part of an animal except its grunt.

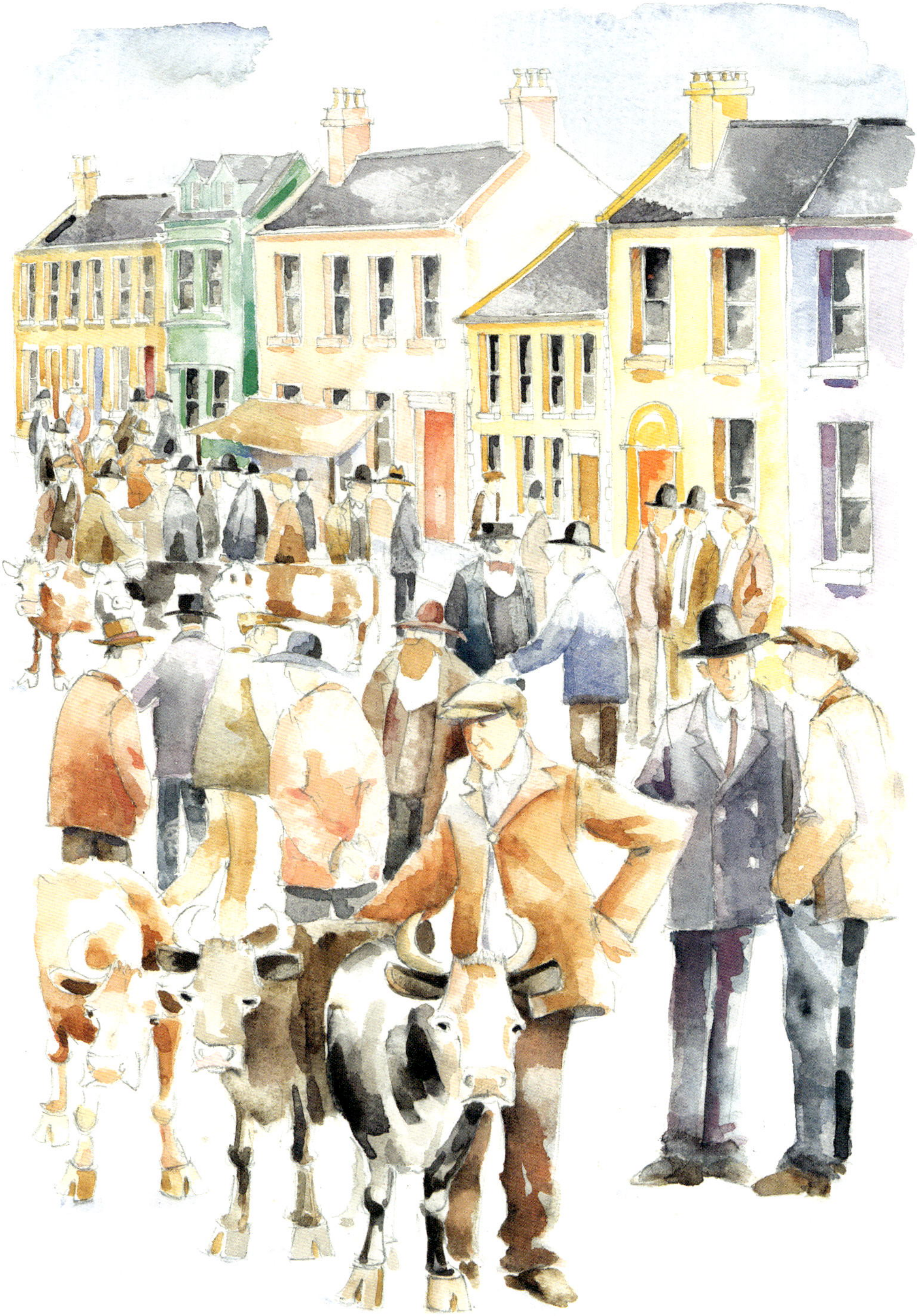

Bealtaine • Mai • Mai

1994   MAY

Monday Luan Montag Lundi • Week 21

16

Tuesday Máirt Dienstag Mardi

17

Wednesday Céadaoin Mittwoch Mercredi

18

Thursday Déardaoin Donnerstag Jeudi

19

Friday Aoine Freitag Vendredi

20

Saturday Satharn Samstag Samedi

21

Sunday Domhnach Sonntag Dimanche

22

FAIR DAY
Belleek, Co. Fermanagh

Belleek, at the western end of County Fermanagh, had three fairs in the 1740s and five by the 1840s. By the 1850s it had a Friday market for six months 'for butter and oats only' but this must have collapsed. In 1887 a local meeting decided to re-establish a monthly fair on the seventeenth of each month. In 1987 a centenary fair was organised by Johnny Cunningham, the local headmaster, and his friends.

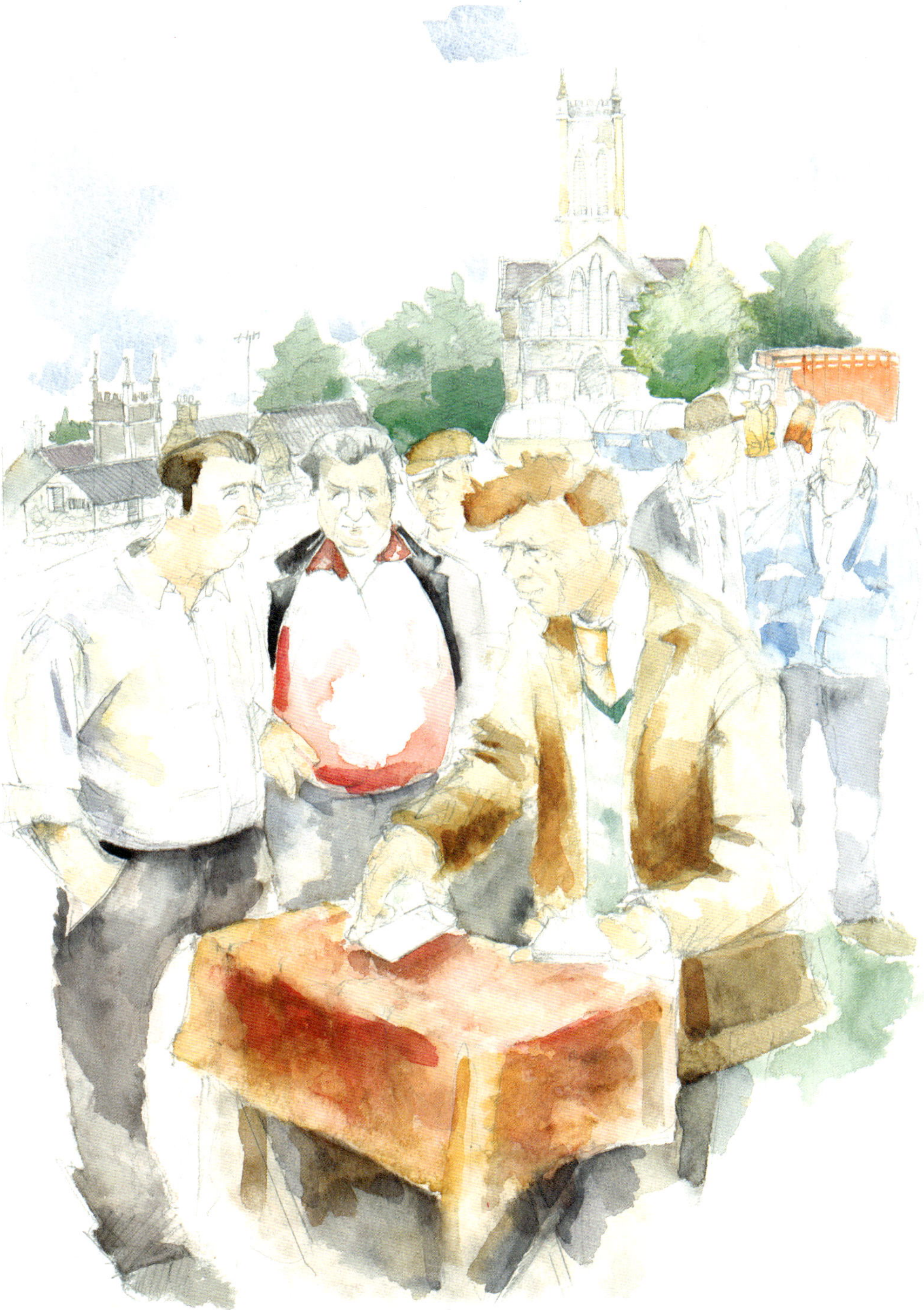

Bealtaine ● Mai ● Mai

1994   MAY

Monday Luan Montag Lundi ● Week 22   **23**

Tuesday Máirt Dienstag Mardi   **24**

Wednesday Céadaoin Mittwoch Mercredi   **25**

Thursday Déardaoin Donnerstag Jeudi   **26**

Friday Aoine Freitag Vendredi   **27**

Saturday Satharn Samstag Samedi   **28**

Sunday Domhnach Sonntag Dimanche   **29**

BALLINASLOE HORSE FAIR
Ballinasloe, Co. Galway

Wherever fools could be parted from their money easily, and especially at fairs, there were specialists to fleece them. The three-card trick man invited customers to turn up the queen among the three cards face down on the table. The thimble rigger challenged them to find the pea under three thimbles. The trick-of-the-loop man wanted them to put a nail in the loop. All very simple.

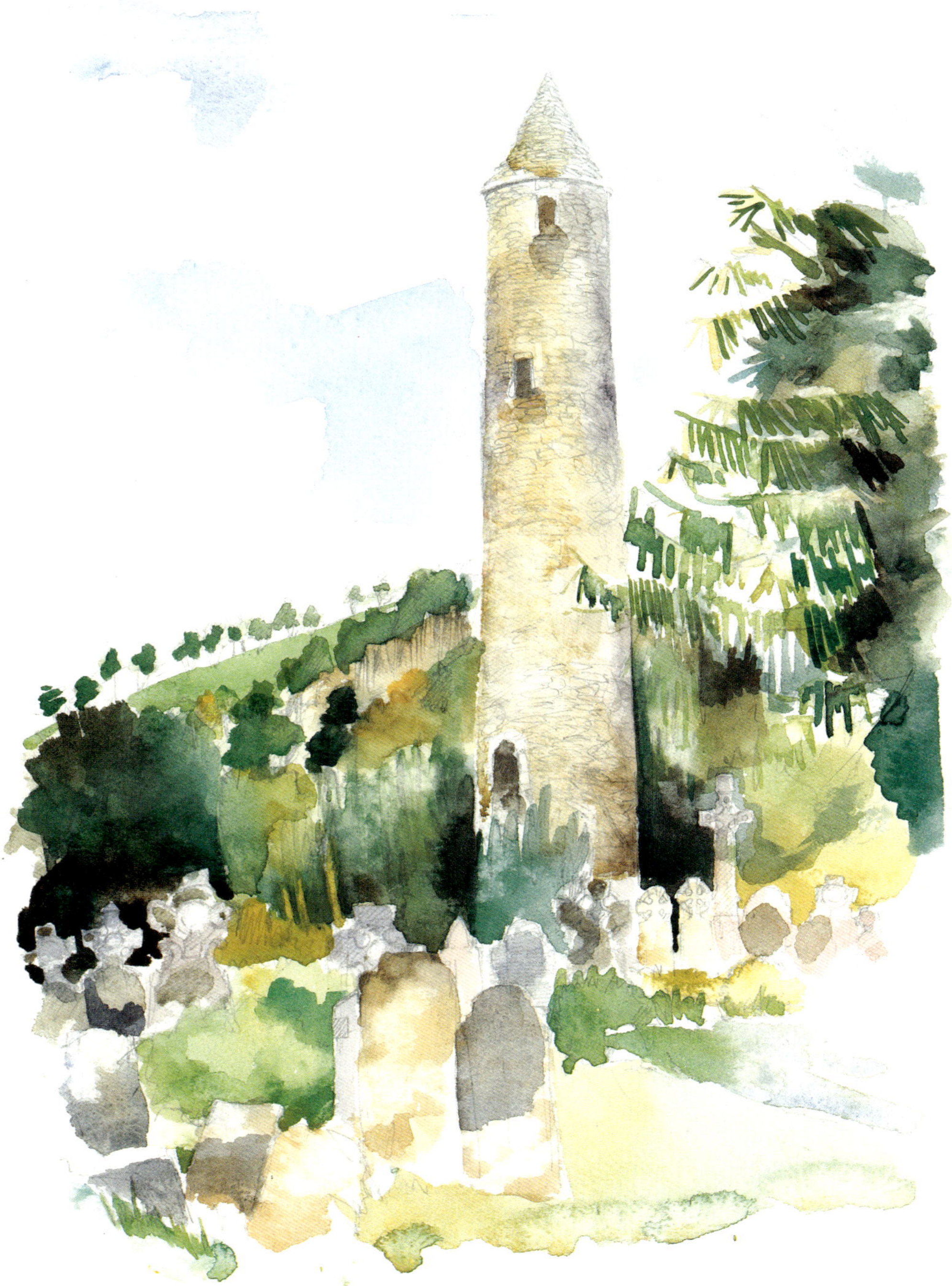

Bealtaine-Meitheamh • Mai-Juni • Mai-Juin

1994 MAY-JUNE

Monday Luan Montag Lundi • Week 23

30

Tuesday Máirt Dienstag Mardi

31

Wednesday Céadaoin Mittwoch Mercredi

1

Thursday Déardaoin Donnerstag Jeudi

2

Friday Aoine Freitag Vendredi

3

Saturday Satharn Samstag Samedi

4

Sunday Domhnach Sonntag Dimanche

5

**GLENDALOUGH
Co. Wicklow**

At Glendalough a 'pattern' or 'patron' used to be celebrated each year on 3 June in honour of St Kevin, the patron saint. This pattern attracted so many dealers in all kinds of goods and services that it was impossible to distinguish in practice between pattern and fair. The pattern of St Kevin was suppressed by Cardinal Cullen in 1862 because faction-fighting and debauchery were bringing religion into disrepute.

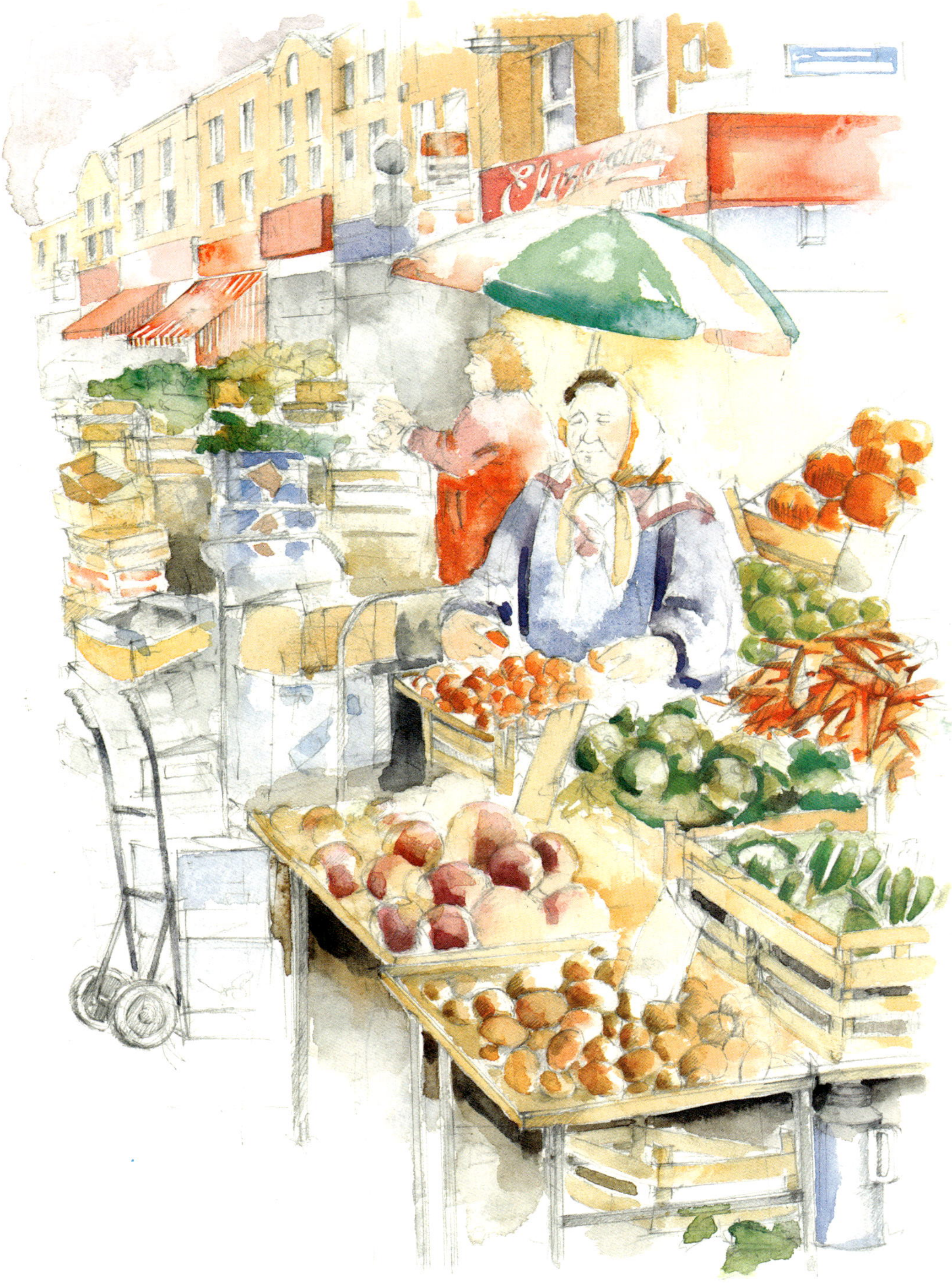

Meitheamh • Juni • Juin

1994   JUNE

Monday Luan Montag Lundi • Week 24
Bank & public holiday

6

Tuesday Máirt Dienstag Mardi

7

Wednesday Céadaoin Mittwoch Mercredi

8

Thursday Déardaoin Donnerstag Jeudi

9

Friday Aoine Freitag Vendredi

10

MOORE STREET MARKET
Moore Street, Dublin

Saturday Satharn Samstag Samedi

11

It is said that street trading in Moore Street began about 1760 and is still buoyant. It has always been dominated by the market women who have succeeded their mothers and their grandmothers. They relish their independence and the social life of the street and have a great reputation for banter and repartee.

Sunday Domhnach Sonntag Dimanche

12

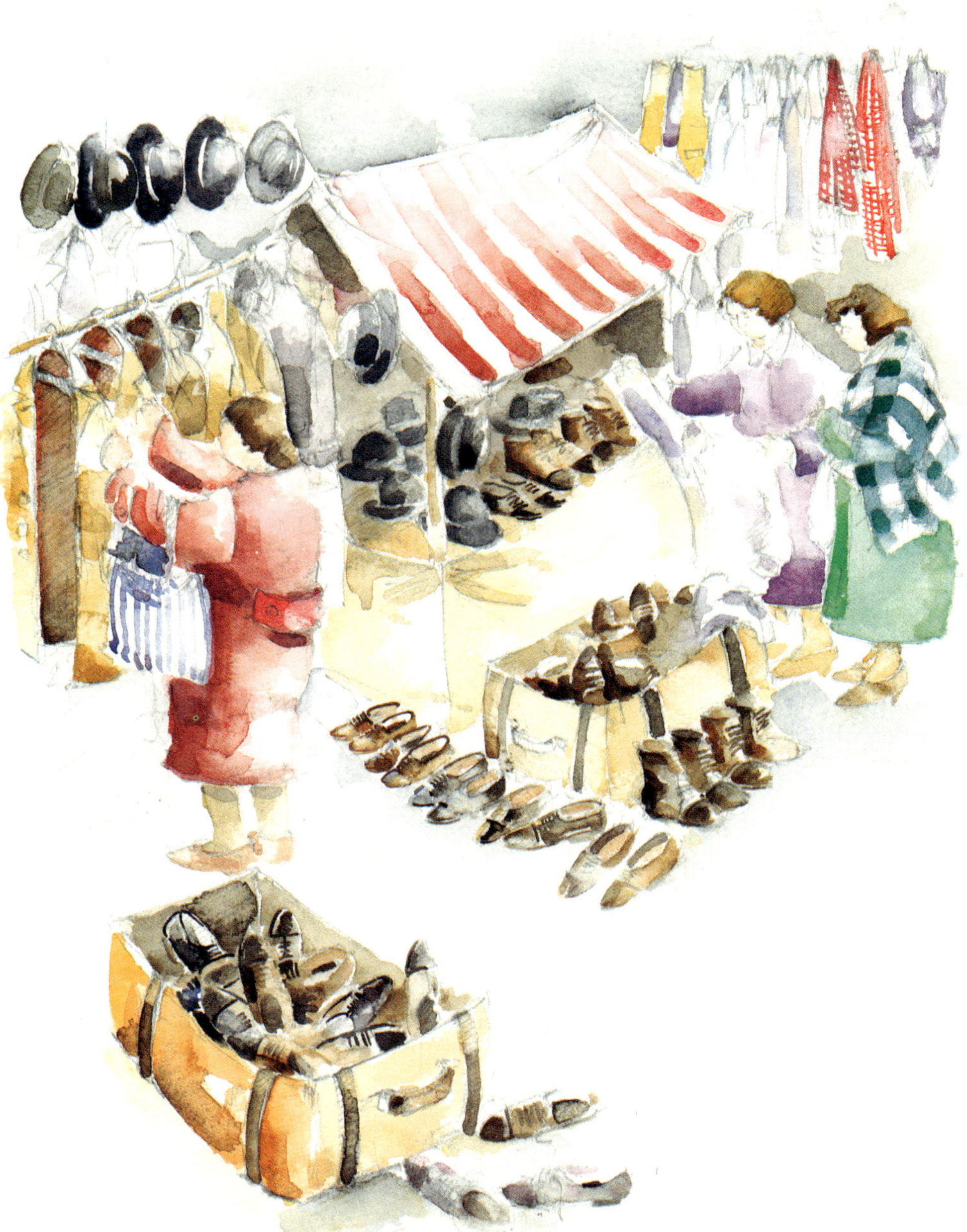

Meitheamh • Juni • Juin

1994   JUNE

Monday Luan Montag Lundi • Week 25   **13**

Tuesday Máirt Dienstag Mardi   **14**

Wednesday Céadaoin Mittwoch Mercredi   **15**

Thursday Déardaoin Donnerstag Jeudi   **16**

Friday Aoine Freitag Vendredi   **17**

Saturday Satharn Samstag Samedi   **18**

Sunday Domhnach Sonntag Dimanche   **19**

CLOTHES MARKET
Belfast

The Clothes Market occupied part of the May's Field complex and overflowed from the busy covered market. The second-hand clothes trade in Ulster has a long history with large consignments regularly imported from Glasgow and Liverpool and retailed at fairs throughout the province. Now it concentrates more on the sale of factory seconds.

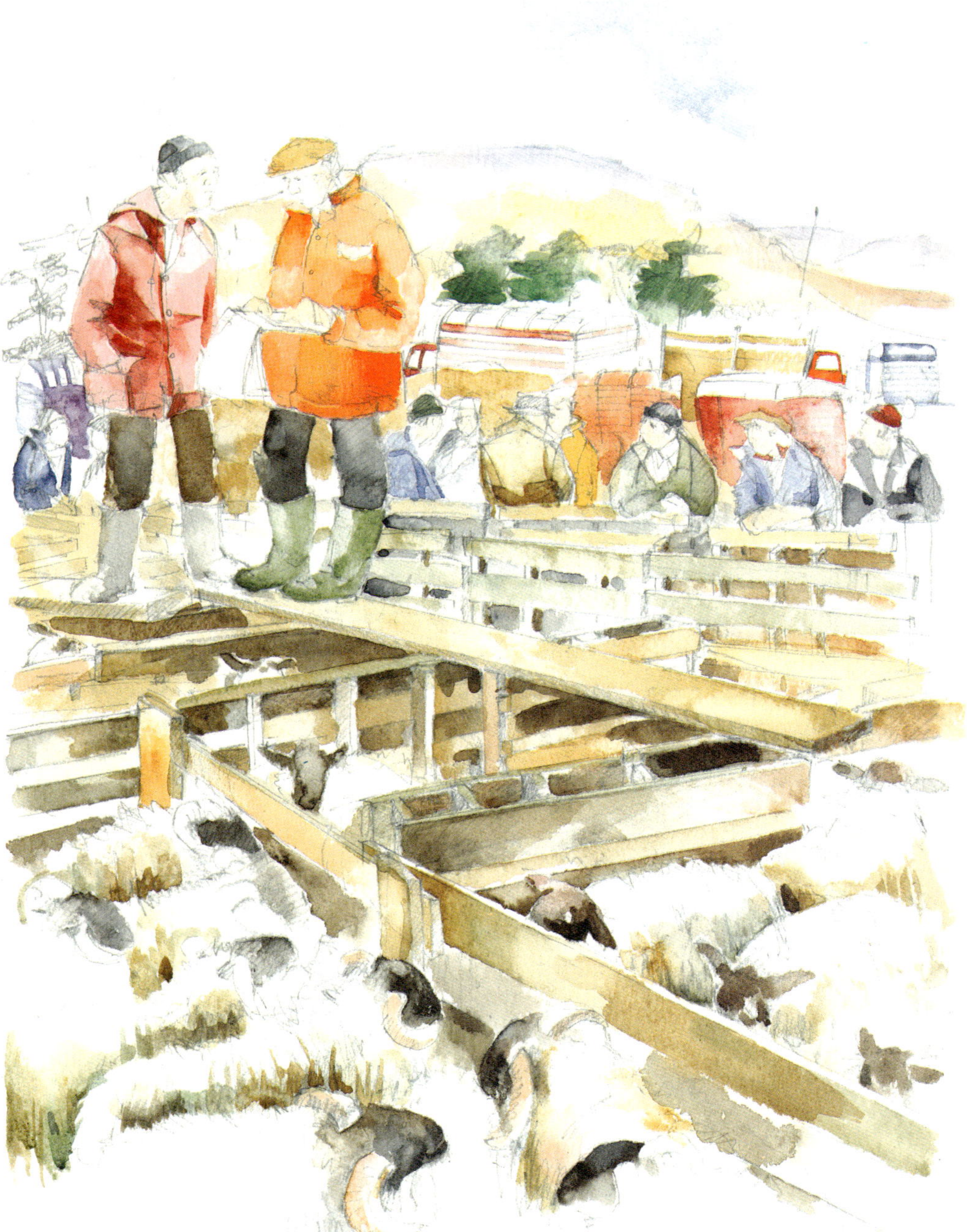

1994 Meitheamh • Juni • Juin
JUNE

Monday Luan Montag Lundi • Week 26
20

Tuesday Máirt Dienstag Mardi
21

Wednesday Céadaoin Mittwoch Mercredi
22

Thursday Déardaoin Donnerstag Jeudi
23

Friday Aoine Freitag Vendredi
24

Saturday Satharn Samstag Samedi
25

Sunday Domhnach Sonntag Dimanche
26

SHEEP AUCTION
Maam Cross,
Co. Galway

After beef-breeders took a serious tumble in living standards in the mid 1970s, sheep-rearers were encouraged by the introduction in 1980 of a beneficial European Community regime. Greater access for Irish sheep meat to the European market boosted a great expansion of sheep production, especially in the hill and upland areas such as Connemara.

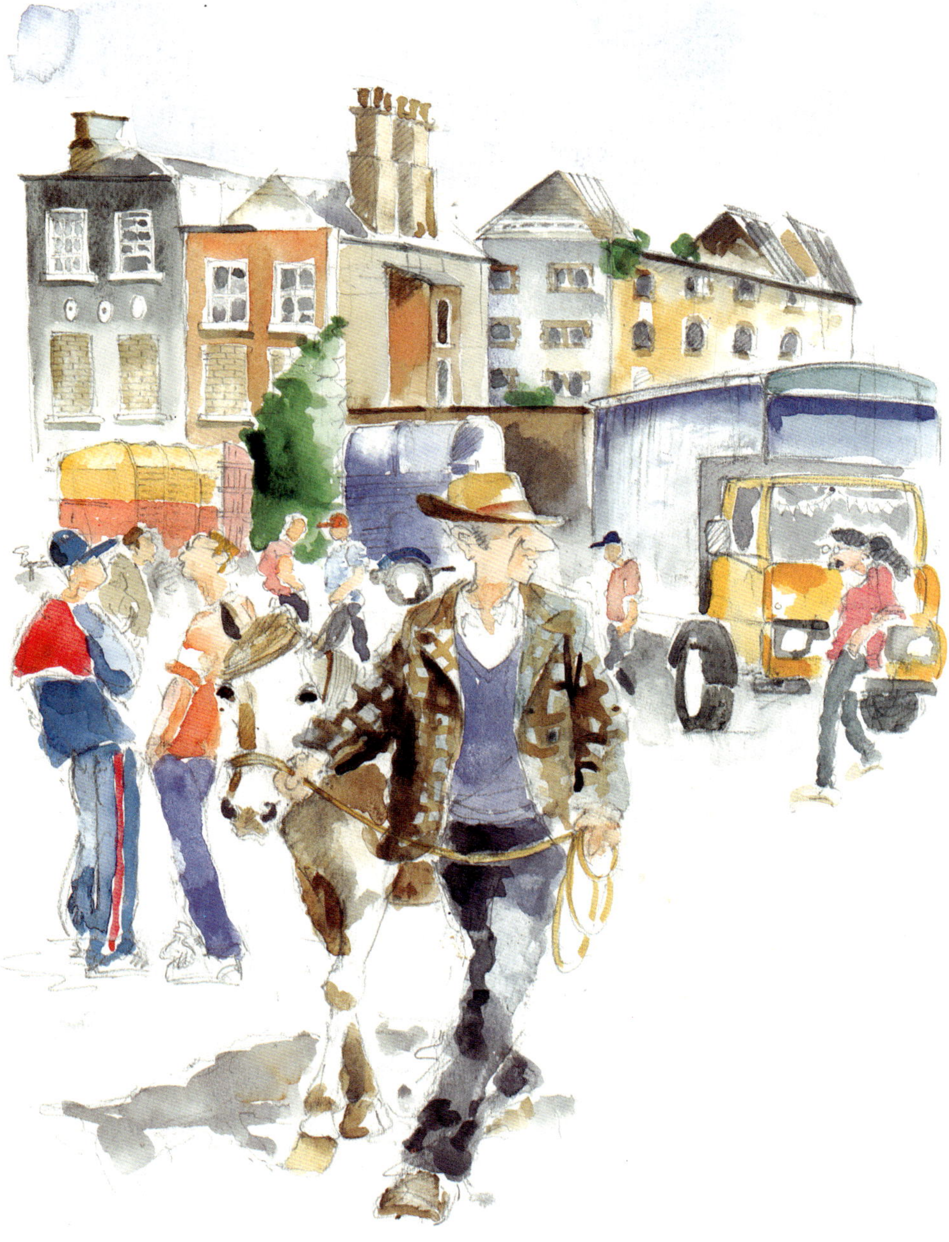

1994 Meitheamh-Iúil • Juni-Juli • Juin-Juillet
JUNE-JULY

Monday Luan Montag Lundi • Week 27

27

Tuesday Máirt Dienstag Mardi

28

Wednesday Céadaoin Mittwoch Mercredi

29

Thursday Déardaoin Donnerstag Jeudi

30

Friday Aoine Freitag Vendredi

1

Saturday Satharn Samstag Samedi

2

Sunday Domhnach Sonntag Dimanche

3

DUBLIN HORSE FAIR
Smithfield, Dublin

The horse fair has always attracted a galaxy of characters, so this gentleman is maintaining a great tradition. He might pride himself about being as knowledgeable and able to show off the good points of a horse as any of the great dealers of the past. His display could produce a fine piece of street theatre.

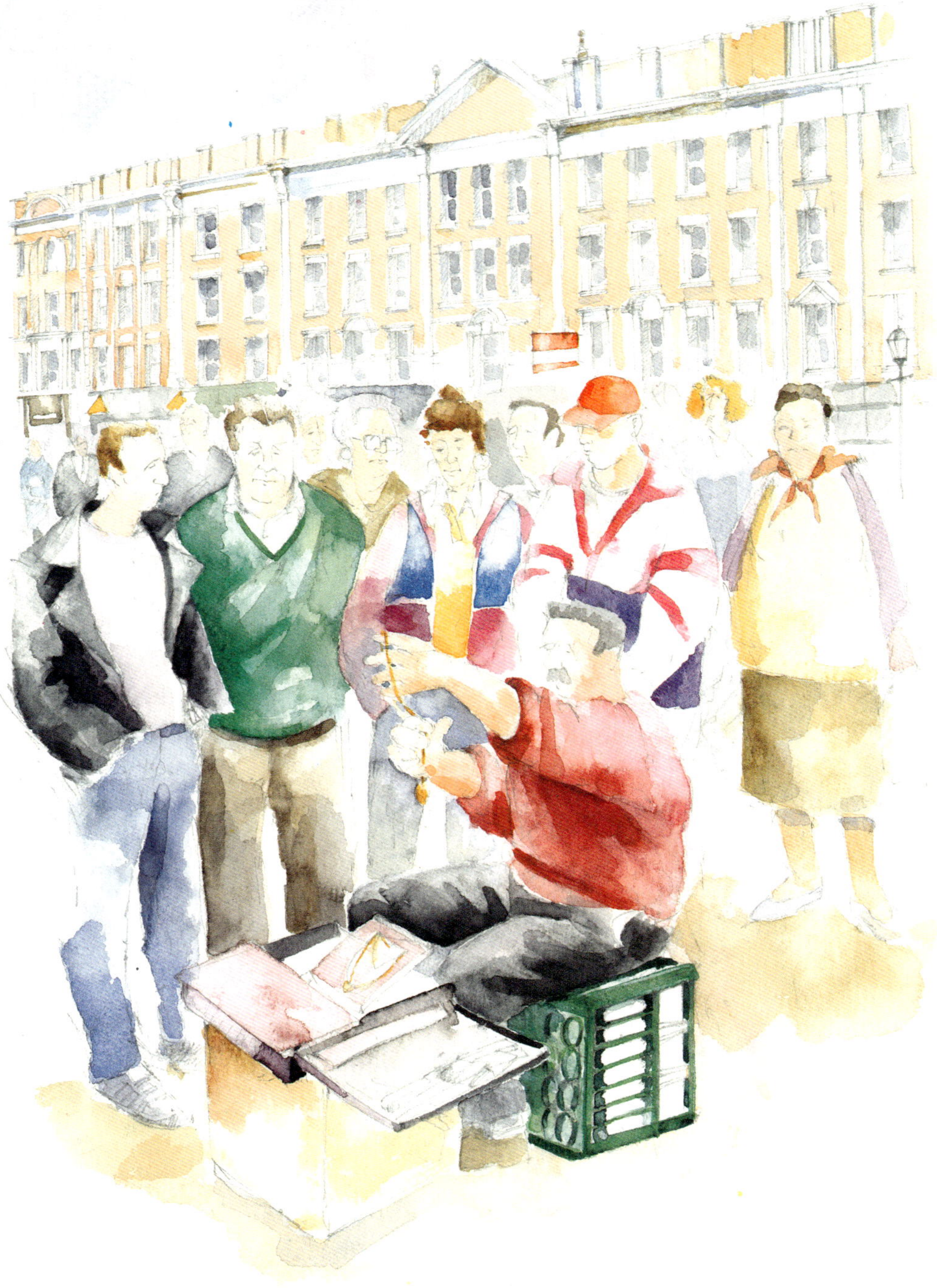

1994

Iúil • Juli • Juillet

JULY

Monday Luan Montag Lundi • Week 28 — **4**

Tuesday Máirt Dienstag Mardi — **5**

Wednesday Céadaoin Mittwoch Mercredi — **6**

Thursday Déardaoin Donnerstag Jeudi — **7**

Friday Aoine Freitag Vendredi — **8**

Saturday Satharn Samstag Samedi — **9**

Sunday Domhnach Sonntag Dimanche — **10**

SPIELER
Henry Street, Dublin

The spieler is one of the most intriguing operators in the Dublin street markets. His distinctive technique is to set up a small stall with his wares and launch into a 'spiel' extolling their quality. They are usually perfume or jewellery which are small, portable and bring a good return. As he operates on the fringe of the law, the spieler has to be able to shut up shop suddenly and disappear into the crowd.

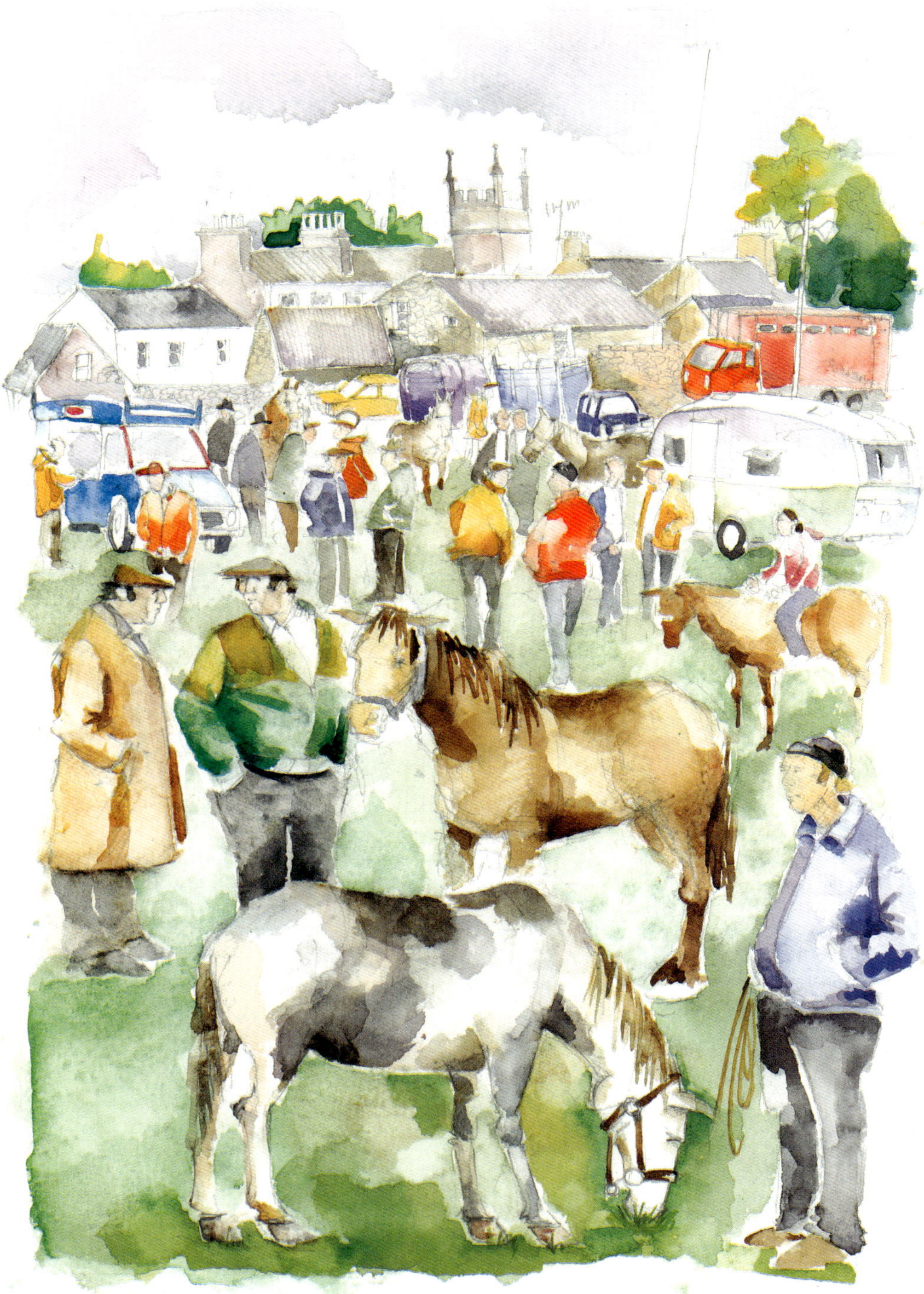

1994

Iúil • Juli • Juillet
JULY

Monday Luan Montag Lundi • Week 29

11

Tuesday Máirt Dienstag Mardi

12

Wednesday Céadaoin Mittwoch Mercredi

13

Thursday Déardaoin Donnerstag Jeudi

14

Friday Aoine Freitag Vendredi

15

Saturday Satharn Samstag Samedi

16

Sunday Domhnach Sonntag Dimanche

17

BALLINASLOE HORSE FAIR
Ballinasloe, Co. Galway

Fairs for sheep, cattle and wool developed at Ballinasloe on the border between the counties of Galway and Roscommon in the mid eighteenth century because Ballinasloe focussed all the traffic from Connacht. In 1853 20,000 cattle and 100,000 sheep were offered for sale. By the twentieth century it became mainly a horse fair patronised by the travelling people.

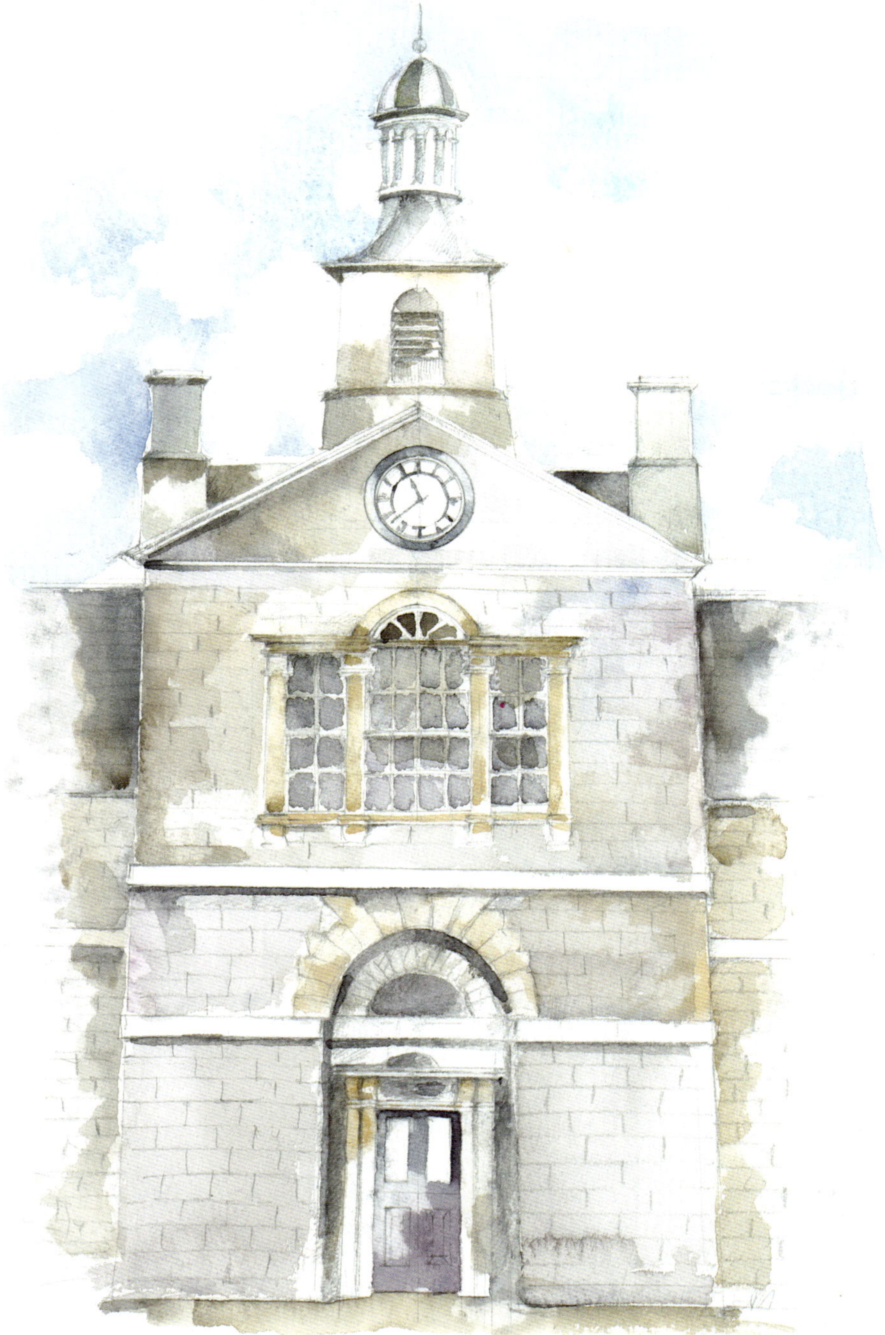

Iúil • Juli • Juillet

1994   JULY

Monday Luan Montag Lundi • Week 30   **18**

Tuesday Máirt Dienstag Mardi   **19**

Wednesday Céadaoin Mittwoch Mercredi   **20**

Thursday Déardaoin Donnerstag Jeudi   **21**

Friday Aoine Freitag Vendredi   **22**

Saturday Satharn Samstag Samedi   **23**

Sunday Domhnach Sonntag Dimanche   **24**

**MARKET-HOUSE
Newtownards,
Co. Down**

This market-house was designed by Ferdinando Stratford of Bristol and was built by the Stewart family (later to be the Marquis of Londonderry) about 1770. Over one wing was the assembly room where fine social occasions were held, while the other wing contained a beautifully furnished drawing-room.

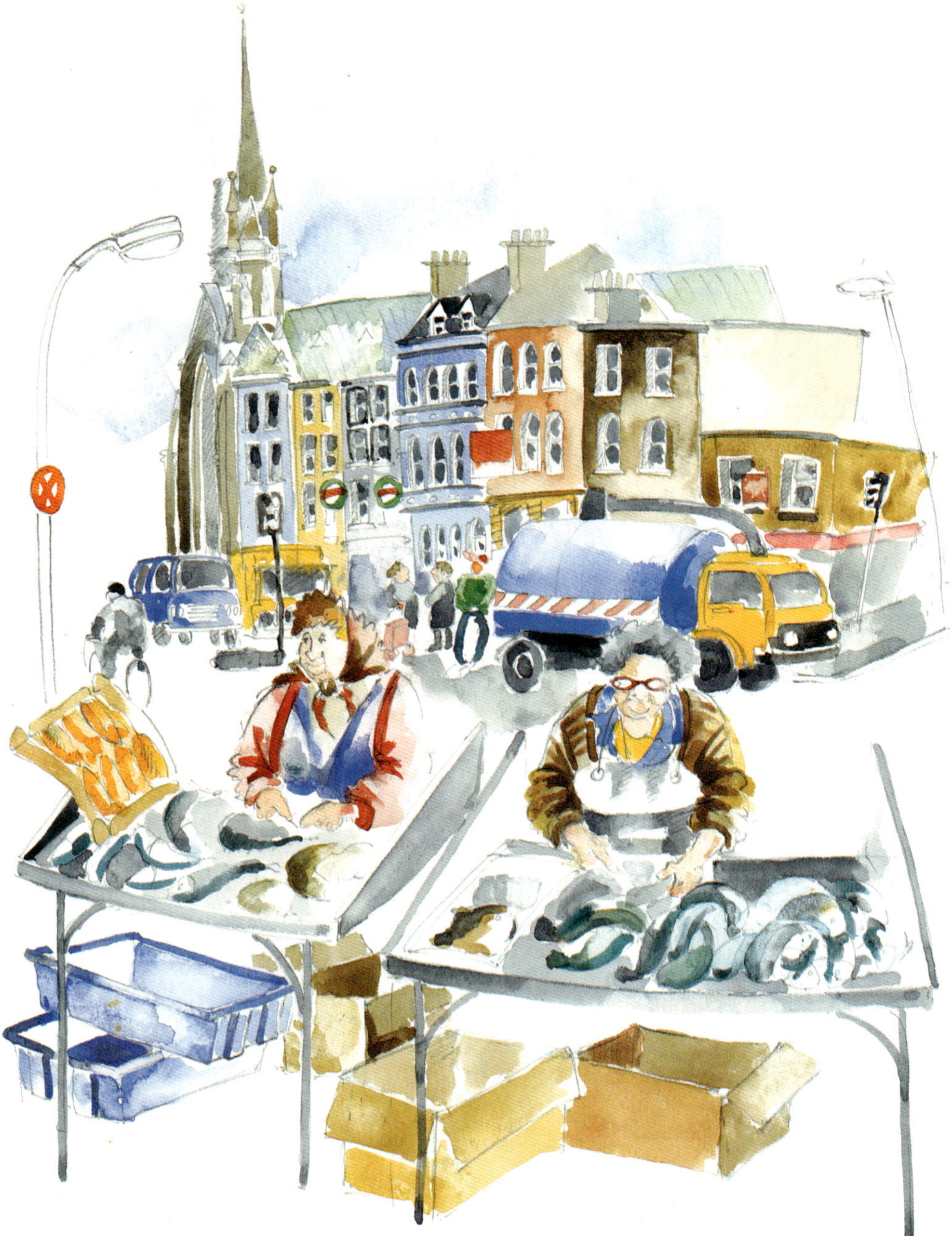

1994　　　　　　　　　　　　　Iúil • Juli • Juillet
JULY

Monday Luan Montag Lundi • Week 31　　**25**

Tuesday Máirt Dienstag Mardi　　**26**

Wednesday Céadaoin Mittwoch Mercredi　　**27**

Thursday Déardaoin Donnerstag Jeudi　　**28**

Friday Aoine Freitag Vendredi　　**29**

Saturday Satharn Samstag Samedi　　**30**

Sunday Domhnach Sonntag Dimanche　　**31**

THOMAS STREET
Dublin

Thomas Street was known for the women selling fish and vegetables. Originally it was St Thomas Street (named after the Abbey of St Thomas founded by King Henry II in atonement for Archbishop Thomas Becket's murder) and it became a major commercial street in the seventeenth century.

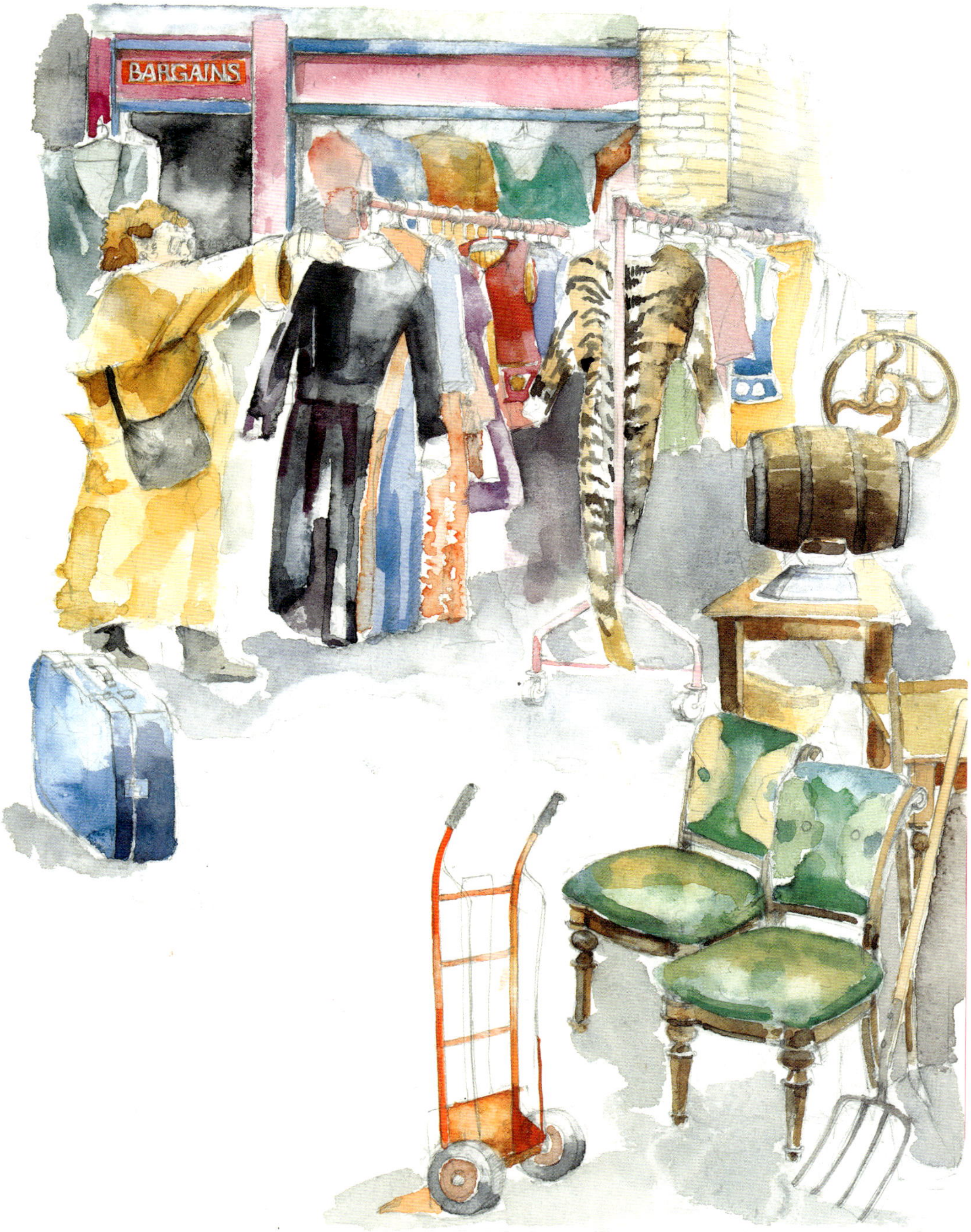
BARGAINS

Lúnasa • August • Août

1994   AUGUST

Monday Luan Montag Lundi • Week 32
Bank & public holiday

1

Tuesday Máirt Dienstag Mardi

2

Wednesday Céadaoin Mittwoch Mercredi

3

Thursday Déardaoin Donnerstag Jeudi

4

Friday Aoine Freitag Vendredi

5

Saturday Satharn Samstag Samedi

6

Sunday Domhnach Sonntag Dimanche

7

BLACKBERRY FAIR
Rathmines, Dublin

Approached through an archway and located behind some Georgian houses on Rathmines Road in this suburb of Dublin, this market held on Saturdays and Sundays recirculates those items that folk consider superfluous.

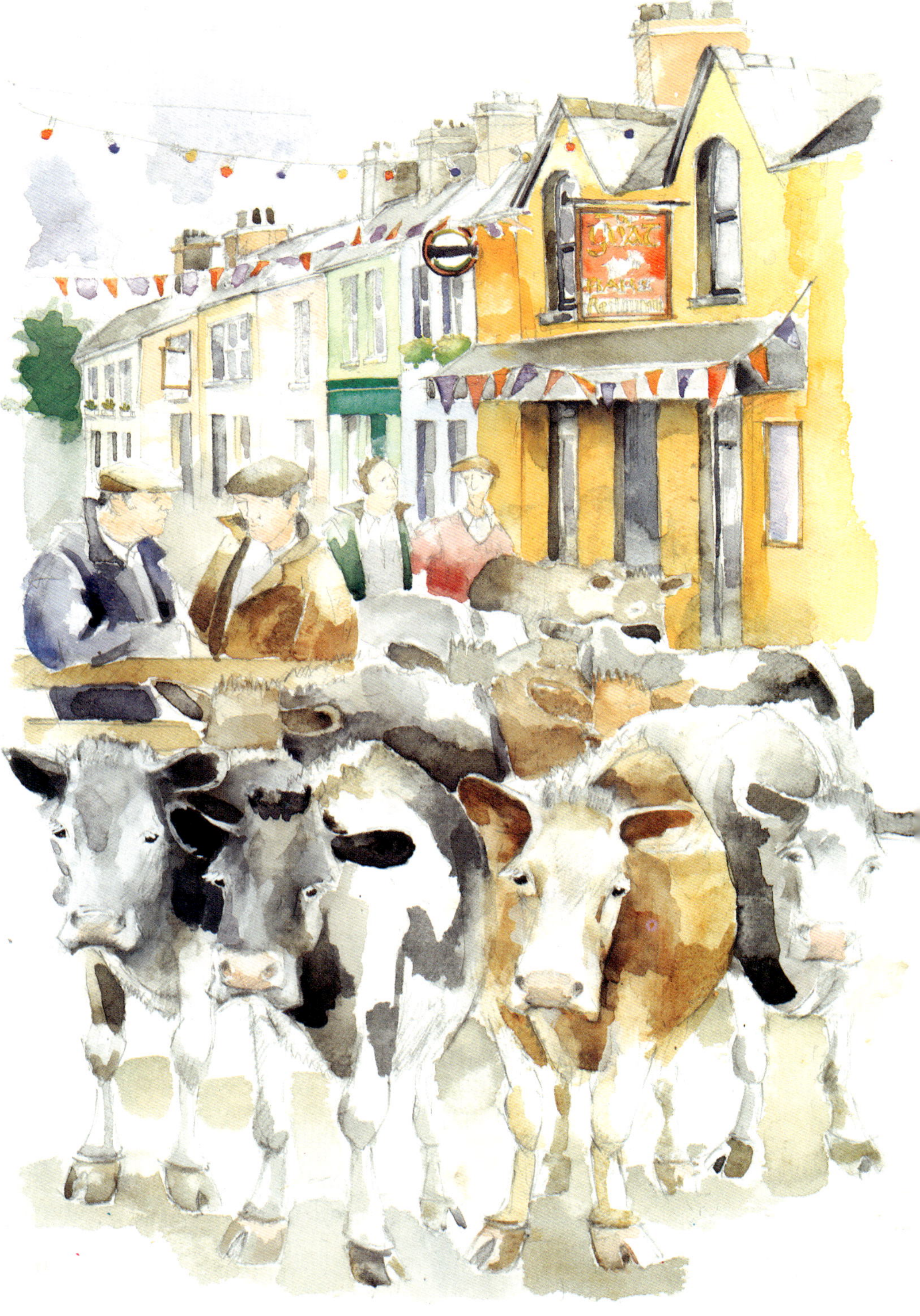

1994

Lúnasa • August • Août

AUGUST

Monday Luan Montag Lundi • Week 33

8

Tuesday Máirt Dienstag Mardi

9

Wednesday Céadaoin Mittwoch Mercredi

10

Thursday Déardaoin Donnerstag Jeudi

11

Friday Aoine Freitag Vendredi

12

PUCK FAIR
Killorglin, Co. Kerry

Locals claim that this three-day fair is 'Ireland's largest and the world's oldest fair'. The excitement it generates reflects the warmth of the community and the puck, or goat, reigns over it. Great stories are told about the origins of the fair but in essence it was one of the Lammas fairs that flourished in a cattle economy.

Saturday Satharn Samstag Samedi

13

Sunday Domhnach Sonntag Dimanche

14

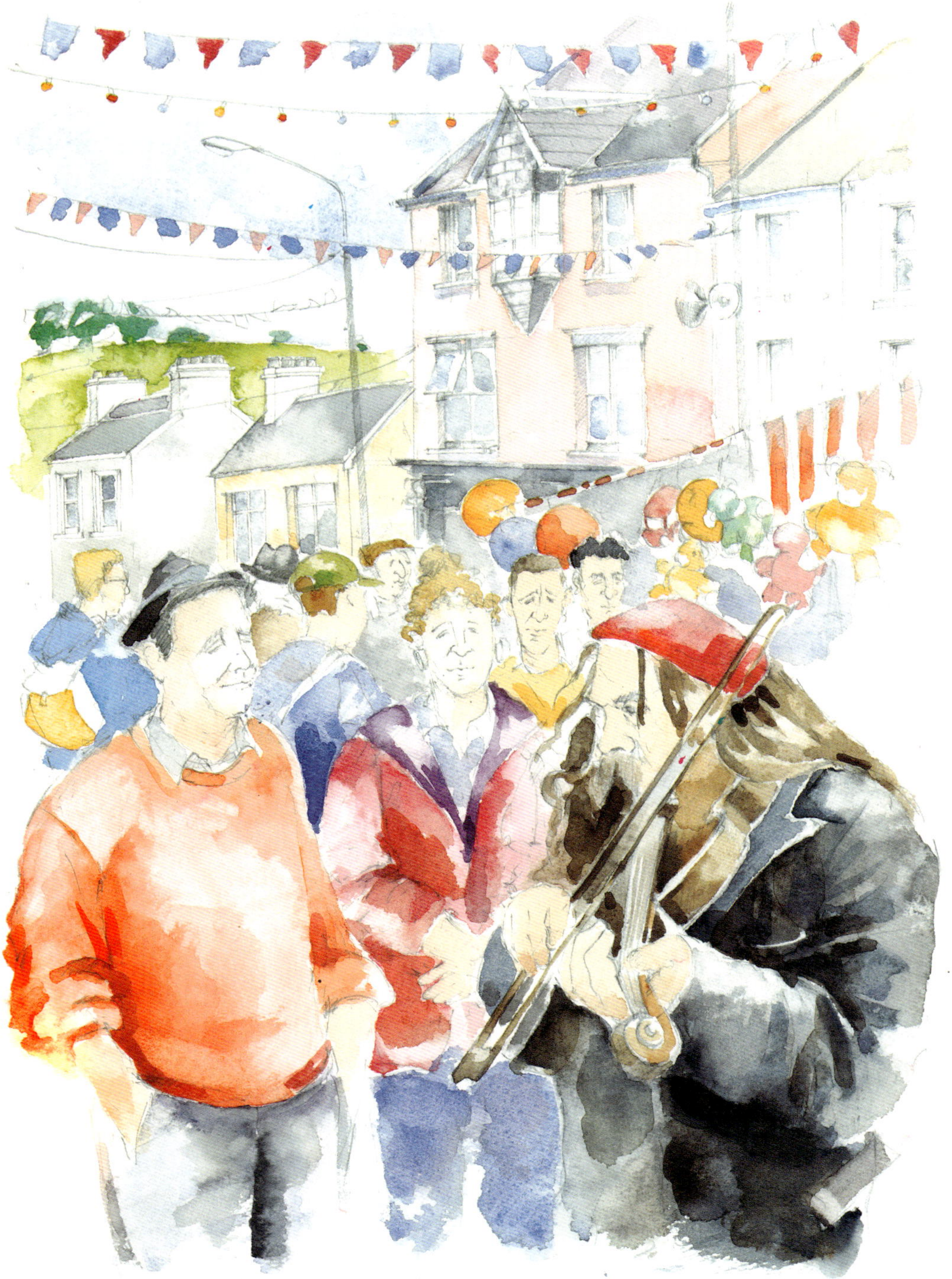

Lúnasa • August • Août

1994 AUGUST

Monday Luan Montag Lundi • Week 34

15

Tuesday Máirt Dienstag Mardi

16

Wednesday Céadaoin Mittwoch Mercredi

17

Thursday Déardaoin Donnerstag Jeudi

18

Friday Aoine Freitag Vendredi

19

Saturday Satharn Samstag Samedi

20

Sunday Domhnach Sonntag Dimanche

21

**PUCK FAIR
Killorglin, Co. Kerry**

The street-musician and the ballad-singer were vital ingredients in every fair. Although the ballad-singer was especially attractive and sold a sheaf of ballads, it was the fiddler or piper who provided the music for the dancers. Dancing was the great pastime for both sexes and in some parts of the country there were regular competitions on the fair days.

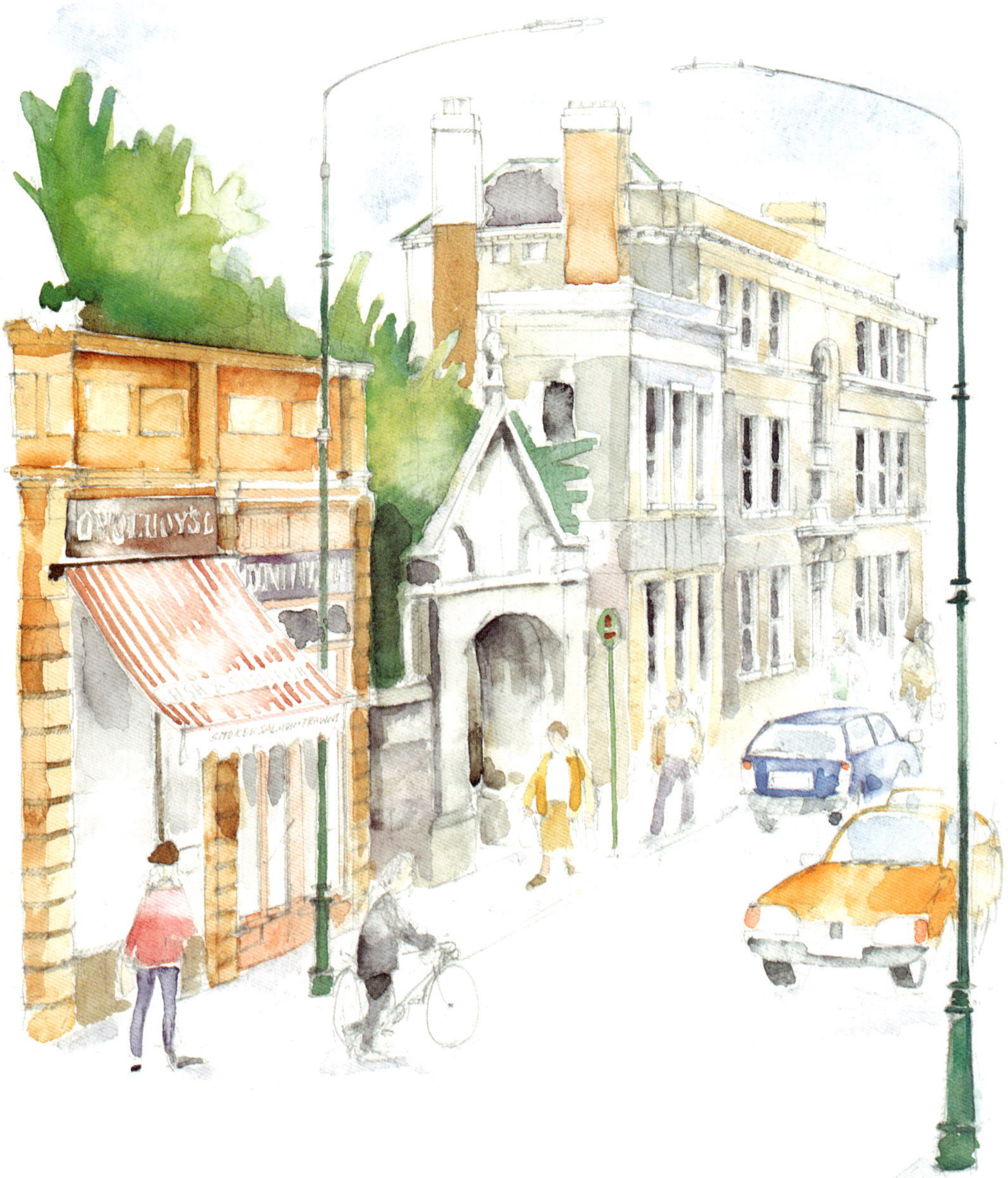
SMOKED SALMON • PRAWNS

Lúnasa • August • Août

1994 AUGUST

Monday Luan Montag Lundi • Week 35

22

Tuesday Máirt Dienstag Mardi

23

Wednesday Céadaoin Mittwoch Mercredi

24

Thursday Déardaoin Donnerstag Jeudi

25

Friday Aoine Freitag Vendredi

26

Saturday Satharn Samstag Samedi

27

Sunday Domhnach Sonntag Dimanche

28

DONNYBROOK
Co. Dublin

This quiet suburb in Dublin was the location of 'that celebrated nuisance, Donnybrook Fair', the most notorious of Irish fairs in the eighteenth century. The patent for this fair was said to have been granted by King John. It commenced on the Monday before 26 August and continued for fifteen days. Although great numbers of stock were bought every year, the principal object was amusement and entertainment.

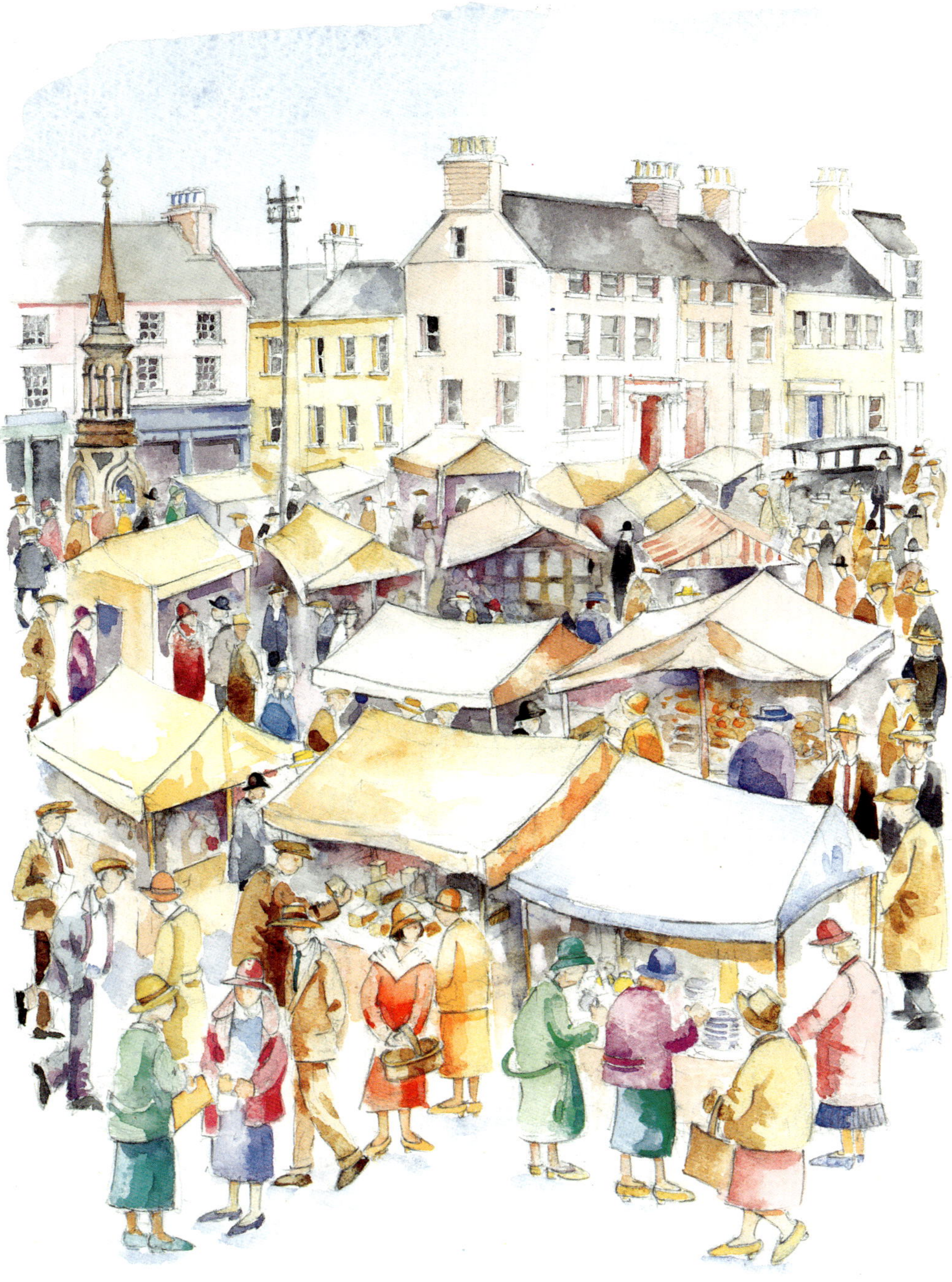

Lúnasa-Meán Fómhair • August-September • Août-Septembre

1994 AUGUST-SEPTEMBER

Monday Luan Montag Lundi • Week 36

29

Tuesday Máirt Dienstag Mardi

30

Wednesday Céadaoin Mittwoch Mercredi

31

Thursday Déardaoin Donnerstag Jeudi

1

Friday Aoine Freitag Vendredi

2

Saturday Satharn Samstag Samedi

3

Sunday Domhnach Sonntag Dimanche

4

THE LAMMAS FAIR
Ballycastle, Co. Antrim

The Lammas Fair at Ballycastle on the North Antrim coast is still held on the last Tuesday in August. There fishermen from Islay and Rathlin rub shoulders with the sheep farmers of the Glens of Antrim. Folk still travel long distances in the expectation of meeting relatives and friends in the fair and they take home the purple edible seaweed known as dulse, and yellowman, a honeycombed sticky toffee.

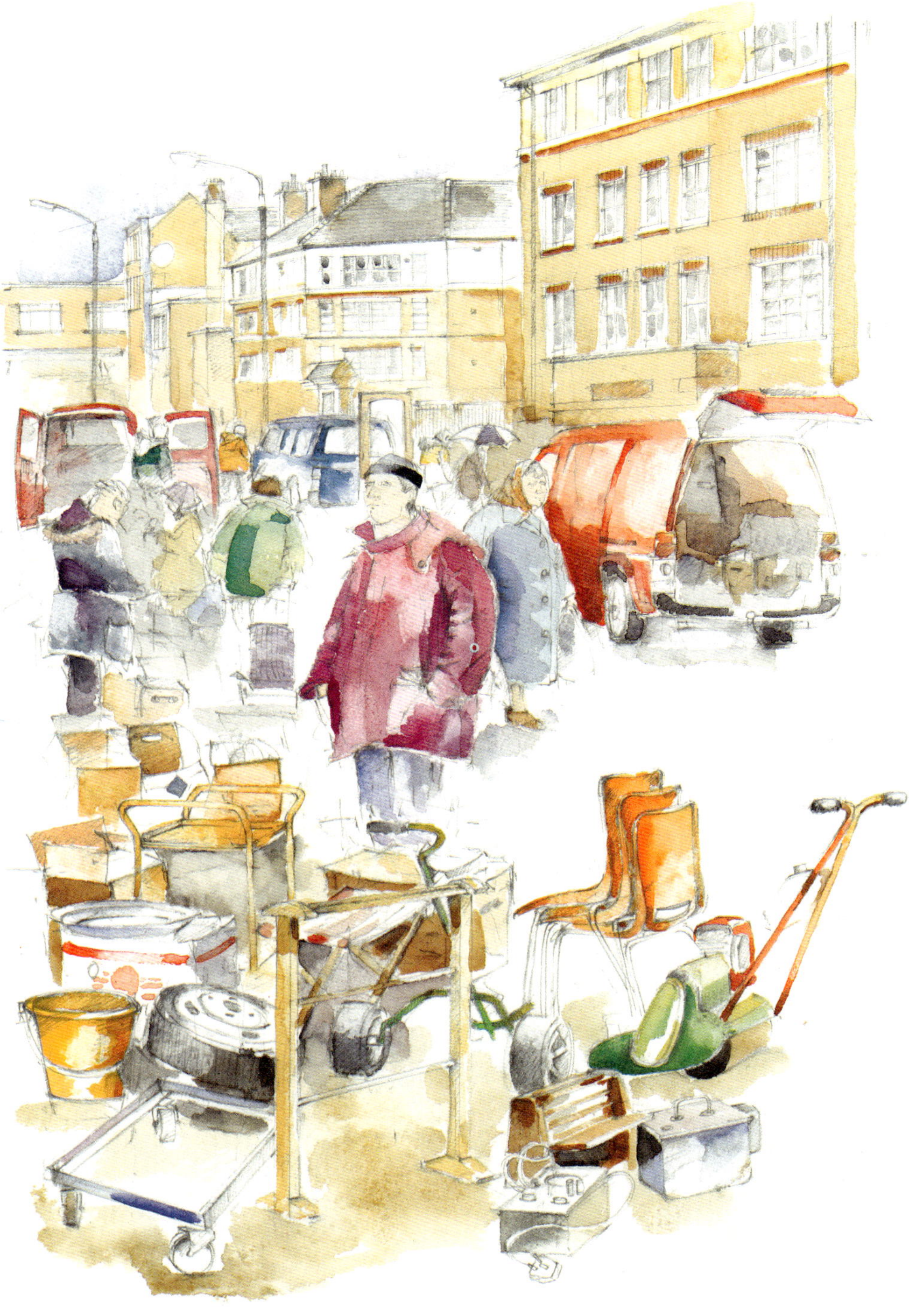

Meán Fómhair ● September ● Septembre

1994 SEPTEMBER

Monday Luan Montag Lundi ● Week 37

5

Tuesday Máirt Dienstag Mardi

6

Wednesday Céadaoin Mittwoch Mercredi

7

Thursday Déardaoin Donnerstag Jeudi

8

Friday Aoine Freitag Vendredi

9

Saturday Satharn Samstag Samedi

10

Sunday Domhnach Sonntag Dimanche

11

CUMBERLAND STREET MARKET
Dublin

When is a car-boot sale a market? This Dublin market is held on Saturday mornings only and there is no sign of stalls: the locals are probably recognising the absence of facilities when they refer to it as 'the Stones'.

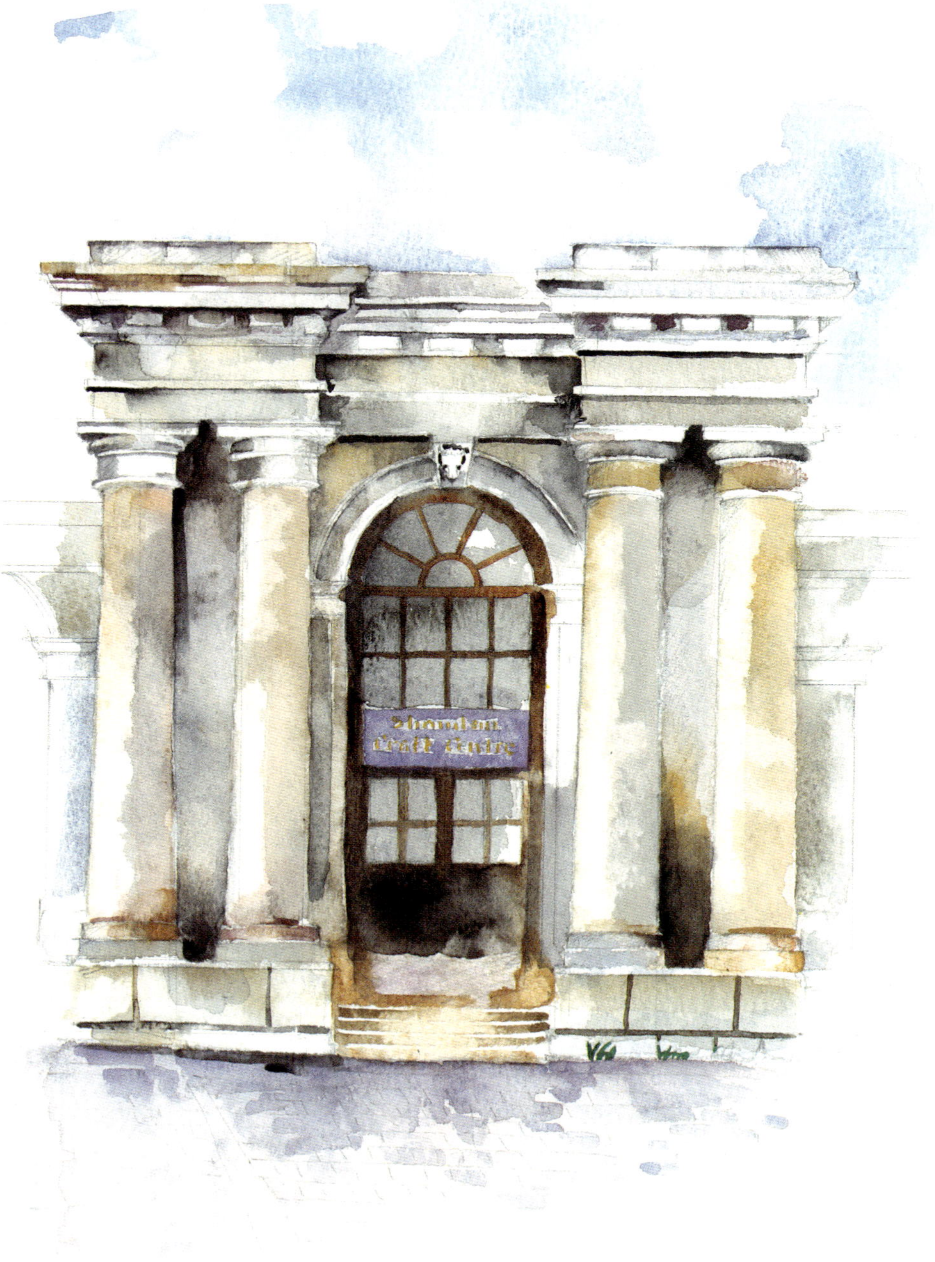

Meán Fómhair ● September ● Septembre

1994 SEPTEMBER

Monday Luan Montag Lundi ● Week 38

12

Tuesday Máirt Dienstag Mardi

13

Wednesday Céadaoin Mittwoch Mercredi

14

Thursday Déardaoin Donnerstag Jeudi

15

Friday Aoine Freitag Vendredi

16

Saturday Satharn Samstag Samedi

17

Sunday Domhnach Sonntag Dimanche

18

FORMER BUTTER EXCHANGE
Cork

About 1770 when Cork and Waterford were responsible for the bulk of Ireland's export of salted butter to the West Indies, the Butter Exchange was founded in Cork. As a result, the Cork Butter Market became the largest of its kind in the British Isles. Until 1884 butter could only be sold in the market when it had been inspected and branded for quality.

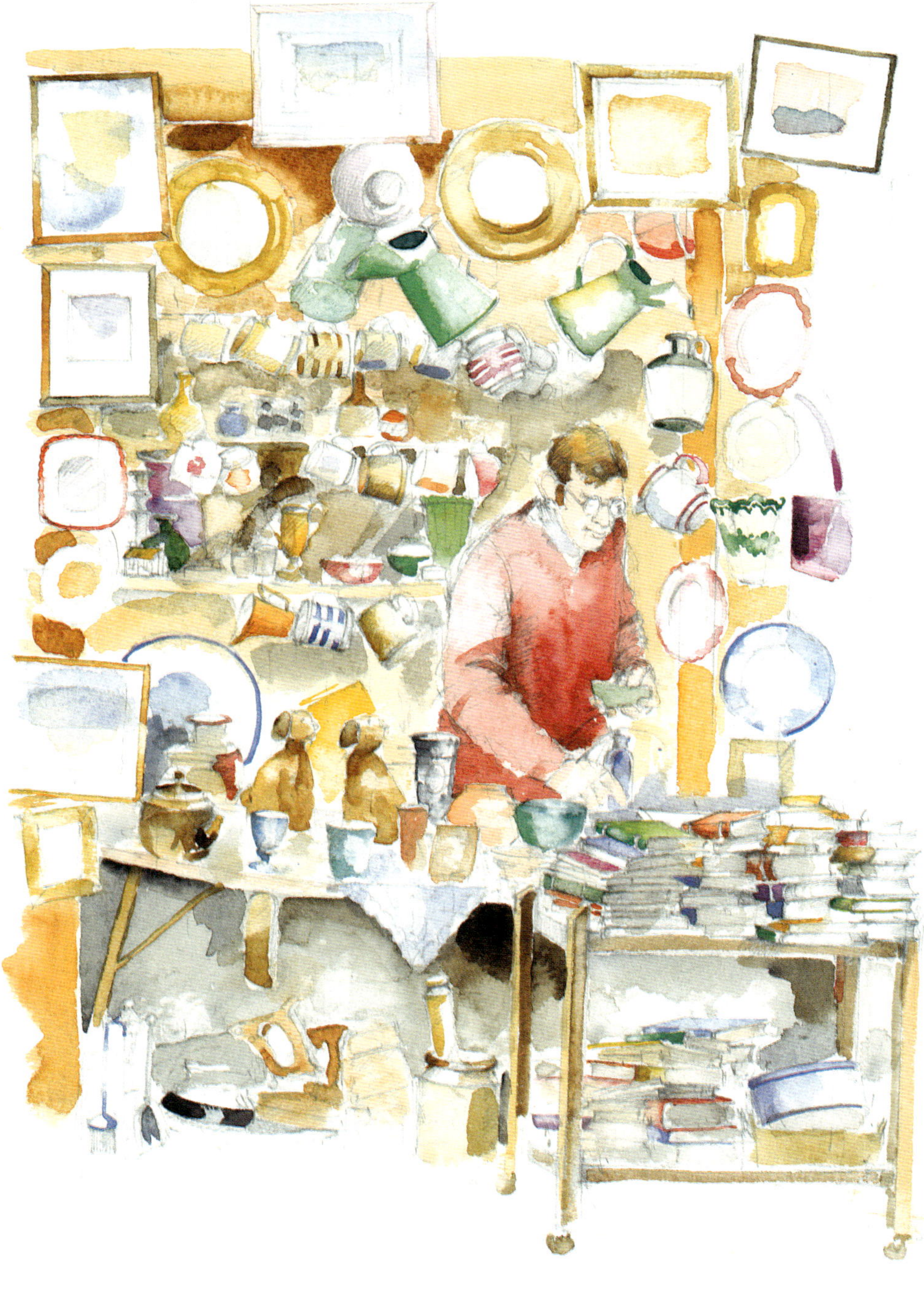

Meán Fómhair • September • Septembre

1994   SEPTEMBER

Monday Luan Montag Lundi • Week 39   **19**

Tuesday Máirt Dienstag Mardi   **20**

Wednesday Céadaoin Mittwoch Mercredi   **21**

Thursday Déardaoin Donnerstag Jeudi   **22**

Friday Aoine Freitag Vendredi   **23**

Saturday Satharn Samstag Samedi   **24**

Sunday Domhnach Sonntag Dimanche   **25**

MOTHER REDCAP'S MARKET
Dublin

Mother Redcap's Market is held on Saturdays and Sundays not far from Christ Church Cathedral. It exists to traffic in the relics of our lives: the sentimental gifts, the mementoes of friends and occasions that mean little to anyone but ourselves.

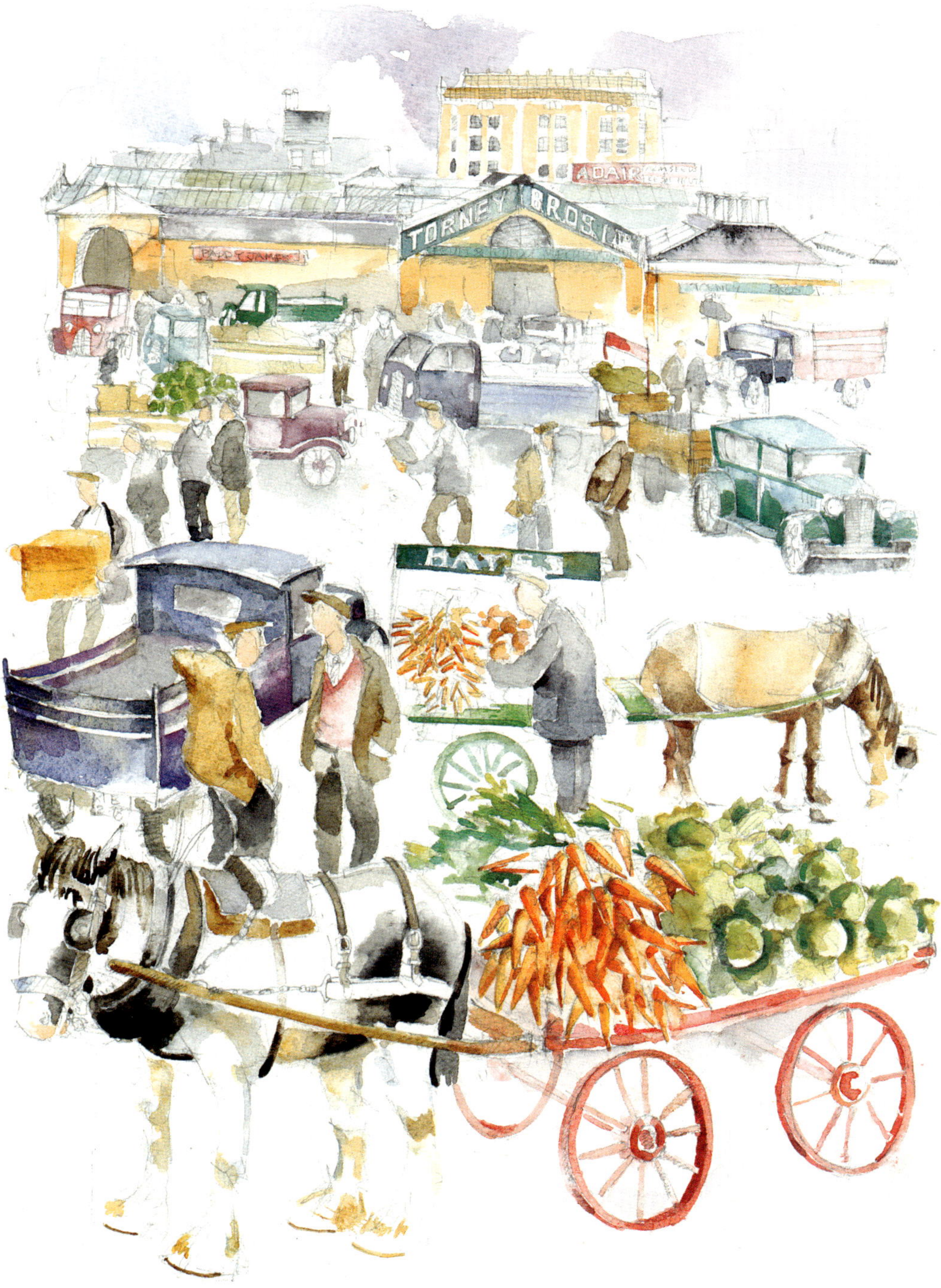
ADAIR
TORNEY BROS. LTD

Meán Fómhair-Deireadh Fómhair • September-Oktober • Septembre-Octobre

1994 SEPTEMBER-OCTOBER

Monday Luan Montag Lundi • Week 40

26

Tuesday Máirt Dienstag Mardi

27

Wednesday Céadaoin Mittwoch Mercredi

28

Thursday Déardaoin Donnerstag Jeudi

29

Friday Aoine Freitag Vendredi

30

Saturday Satharn Samstag Samedi

1

Sunday Domhnach Sonntag Dimanche

2

**VEGETABLE MARKET
Belfast**

This extensive market, now being redeveloped, comprised only a small proportion of the markets purchased and developed by the new Belfast Corporation in the 1840s. In 1859 a government commission complimented it for its foresight in purchasing not only the existing markets but also an area of 41.5 acres known as May's Fields. On it they built St George's Market, the Pork Market, the Vegetable Market, the Horse Fair Green, the wholesale Flax and Fruit Market, the retail Fruit Market, and the Cattle Market, 'leaving ample ground for the erection of gas works and slaughter houses'.

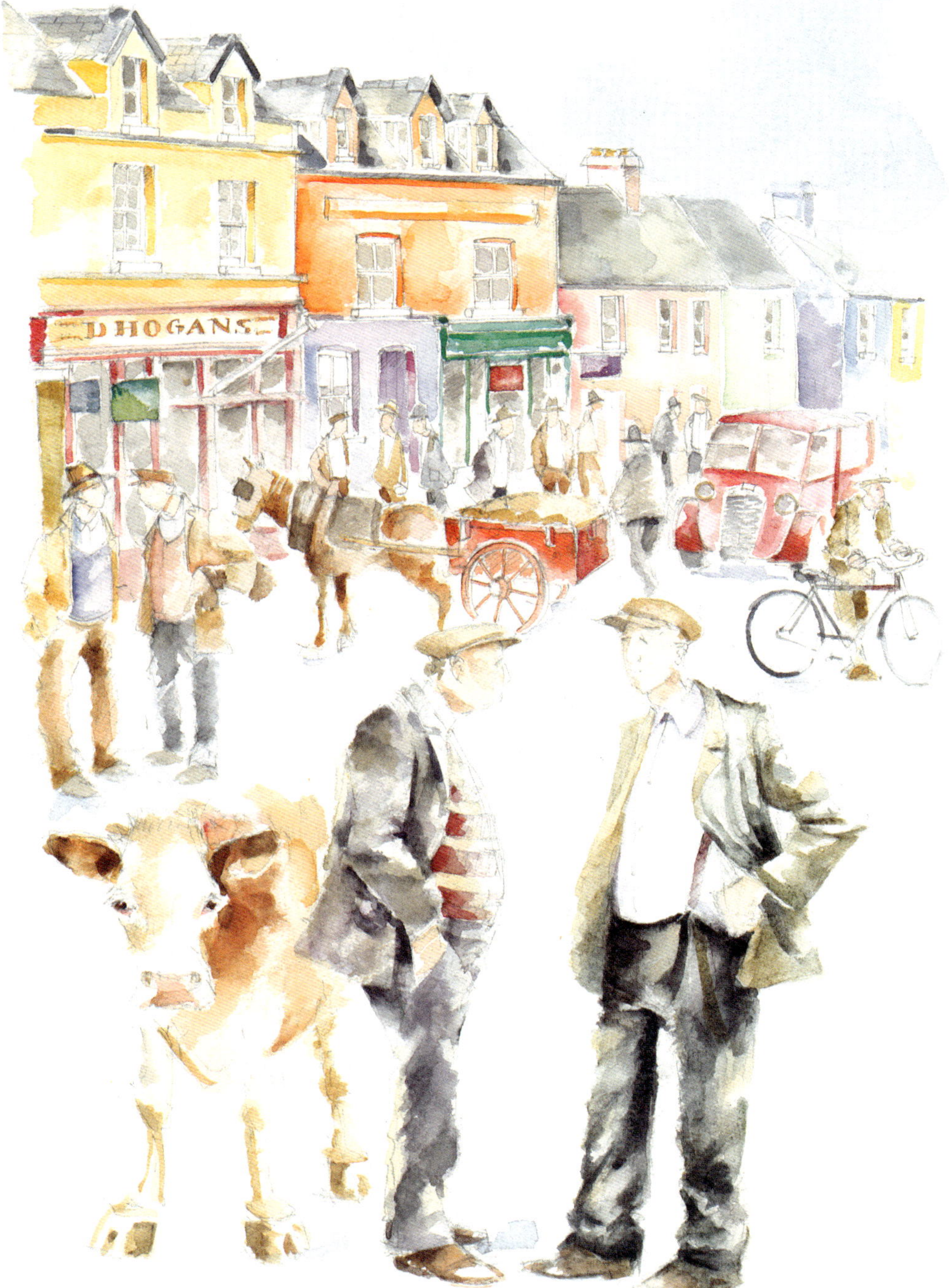
D HOGANS

Deireadh Fómhair ● Oktober ● Octobre

1994   OCTOBER

Monday Luan Montag Lundi ● Week 41

3

Tuesday Máirt Dienstag Mardi

4

Wednesday Céadaoin Mittwoch Mercredi

5

Thursday Déardaoin Donnerstag Jeudi

6

Friday Aoine Freitag Vendredi

7

Saturday Satharn Samstag Samedi

8

Sunday Domhnach Sonntag Dimanche

9

**BALLYGAWLEY
Co. Tyrone**

Ballygawley is a small market-town in County Tyrone that grew up on the main road from Dublin to Derry. Even before the Great Famine it had a regular Friday market. The fairs on the second Friday of the month were for the sale of cattle, sheep and pigs.

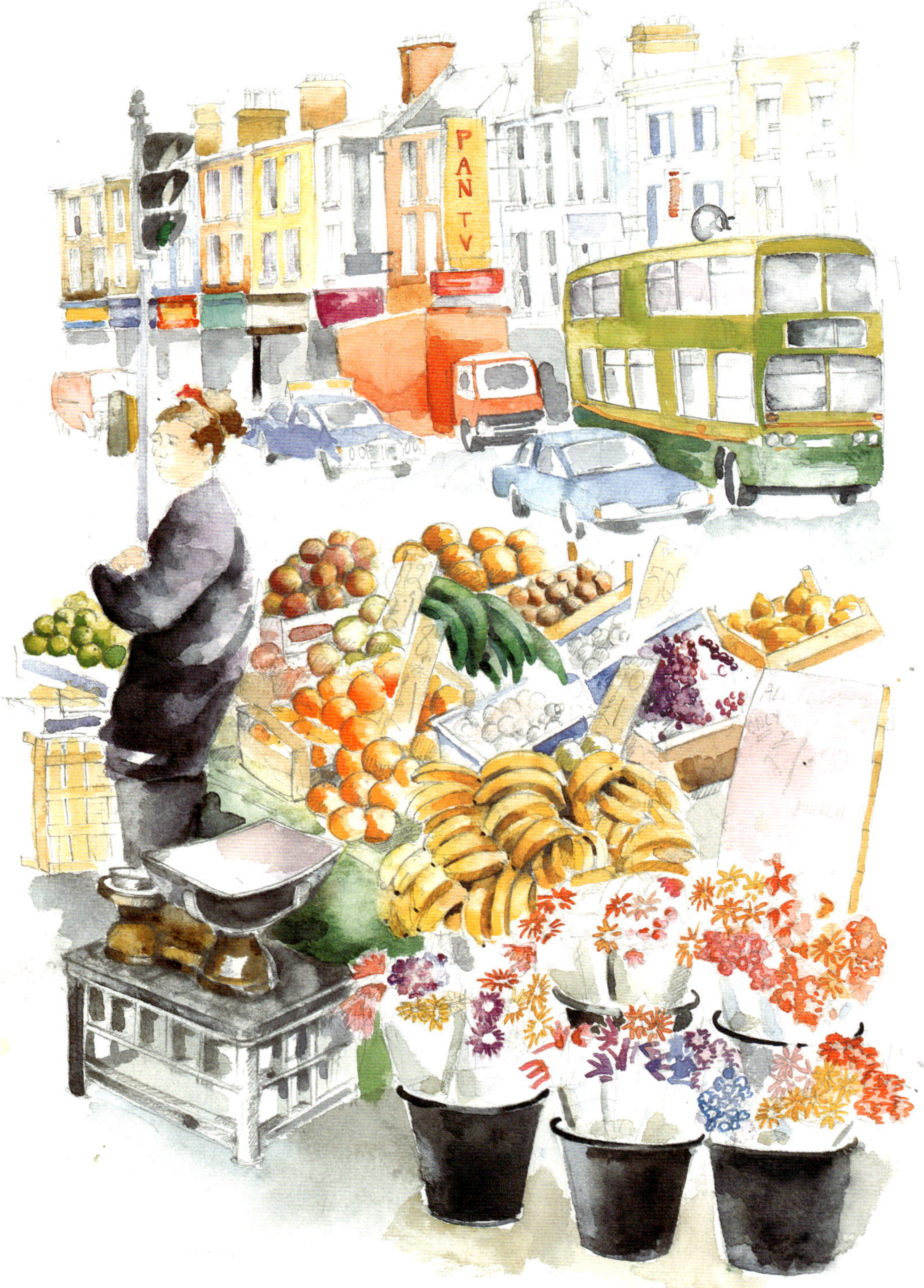
PAN TV

Deireadh Fómhair • Oktober • Octobre

1994   OCTOBER

Monday Luan Montag Lundi • Week 42   **10**

Tuesday Máirt Dienstag Mardi   **11**

Wednesday Céadaoin Mittwoch Mercredi   **12**

Thursday Déardaoin Donnerstag Jeudi   **13**

Friday Aoine Freitag Vendredi   **14**

Saturday Satharn Samstag Samedi   **15**

Sunday Domhnach Sonntag Dimanche   **16**

CAMDEN STREET MARKET
Dublin

A retail market for fruit and vegetables. It is interesting to speculate how this market came to be located here. Not far distant is Kevin Street, which was at one time a major market for bacon, butter, potatoes and hay. The predecessors of the Camden Street traders may have been displaced from Kevin Street.

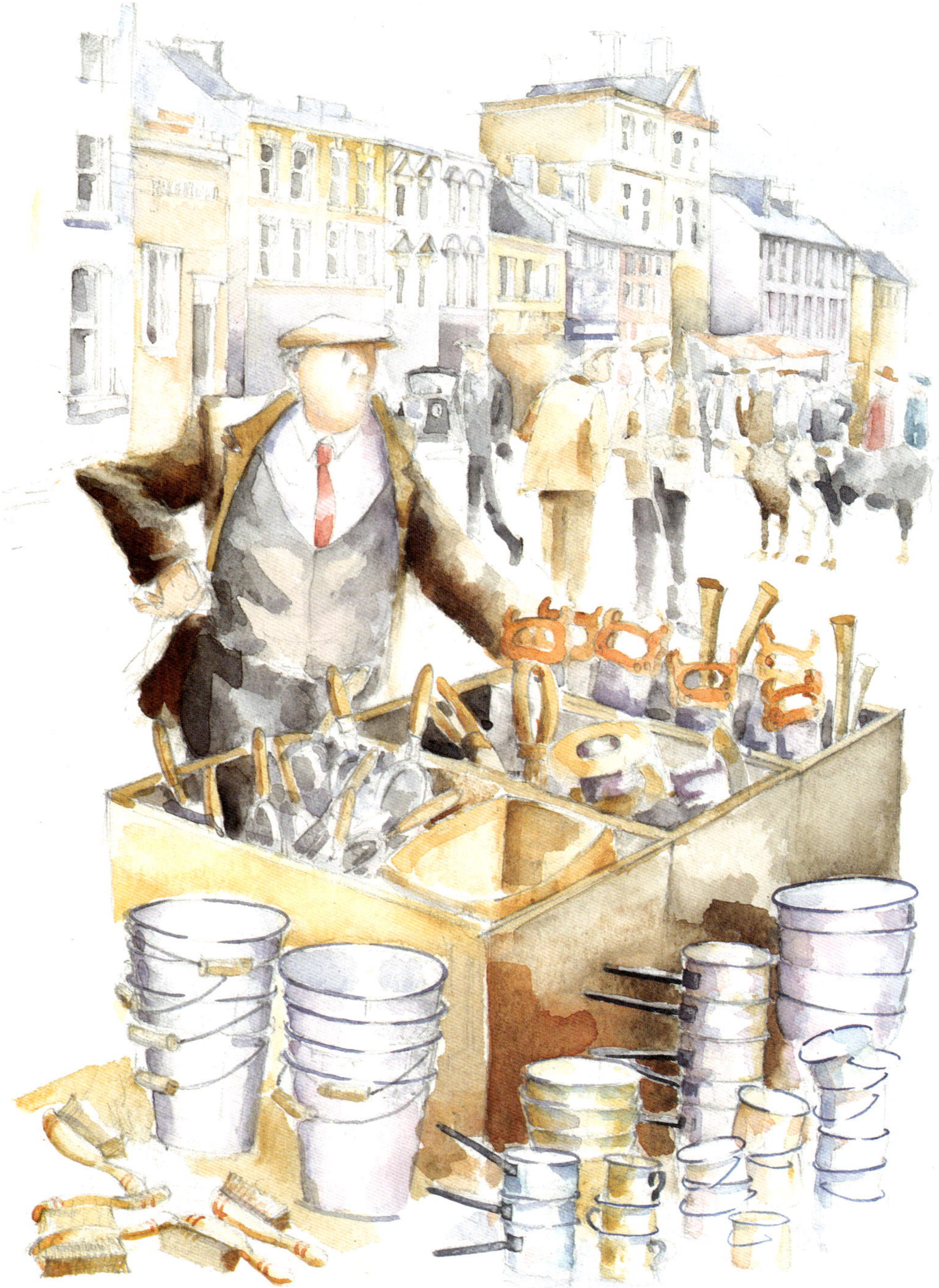

Deireadh Fómhair • Oktober • Octobre

1994 OCTOBER

Monday Luan Montag Lundi • Week 43

17

Tuesday Máirt Dienstag Mardi

18

Wednesday Céadaoin Mittwoch Mercredi

19

Thursday Déardaoin Donnerstag Jeudi

20

Friday Aoine Freitag Vendredi

21

Saturday Satharn Samstag Samedi

22

Sunday Domhnach Sonntag Dimanche

23

FAIR DAY
Longford, Co. Longford

Much of the tinware used in the countryside was made by the tinkers, as the travelling people were known. Although their skills in making and mending were invaluable during the Second World War, they posed no long-term threat to the dealers who transported household wares from fair to fair.

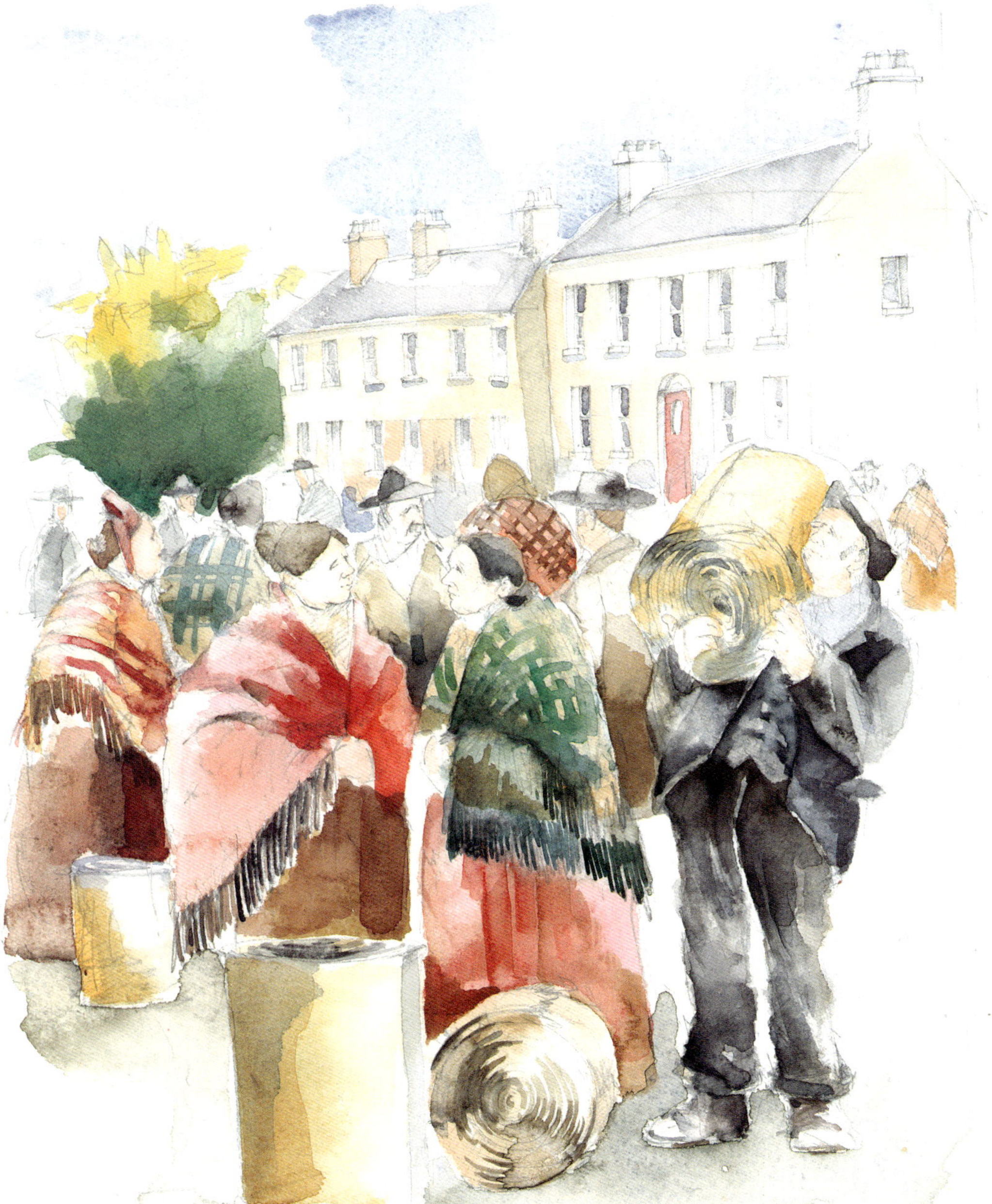

1994　　　　　　　Deireadh Fómhair ● Oktober ● Octobre
OCTOBER

Monday Luan Montag Lundi ● Week 44

24

Tuesday Máirt Dienstag Mardi

25

Wednesday Céadaoin Mittwoch Mercredi

26

Thursday Déardaoin Donnerstag Jeudi

27

Friday Aoine Freitag Vendredi

28

Saturday Satharn Samstag Samedi

29

Sunday Domhnach Sonntag Dimanche

30

**ARDARA
Co. Donegal**

Although the Ardara district of South Donegal had a tradition of weaving homespuns before the Great Famine, the industry did not become commercial until the final years of the nineteenth century. The tweed industry was promoted first by the Donegal Industrial Fund and then by the Congested Districts Board which supervised quality by inspecting the webs before the Fair Day in Ardara.

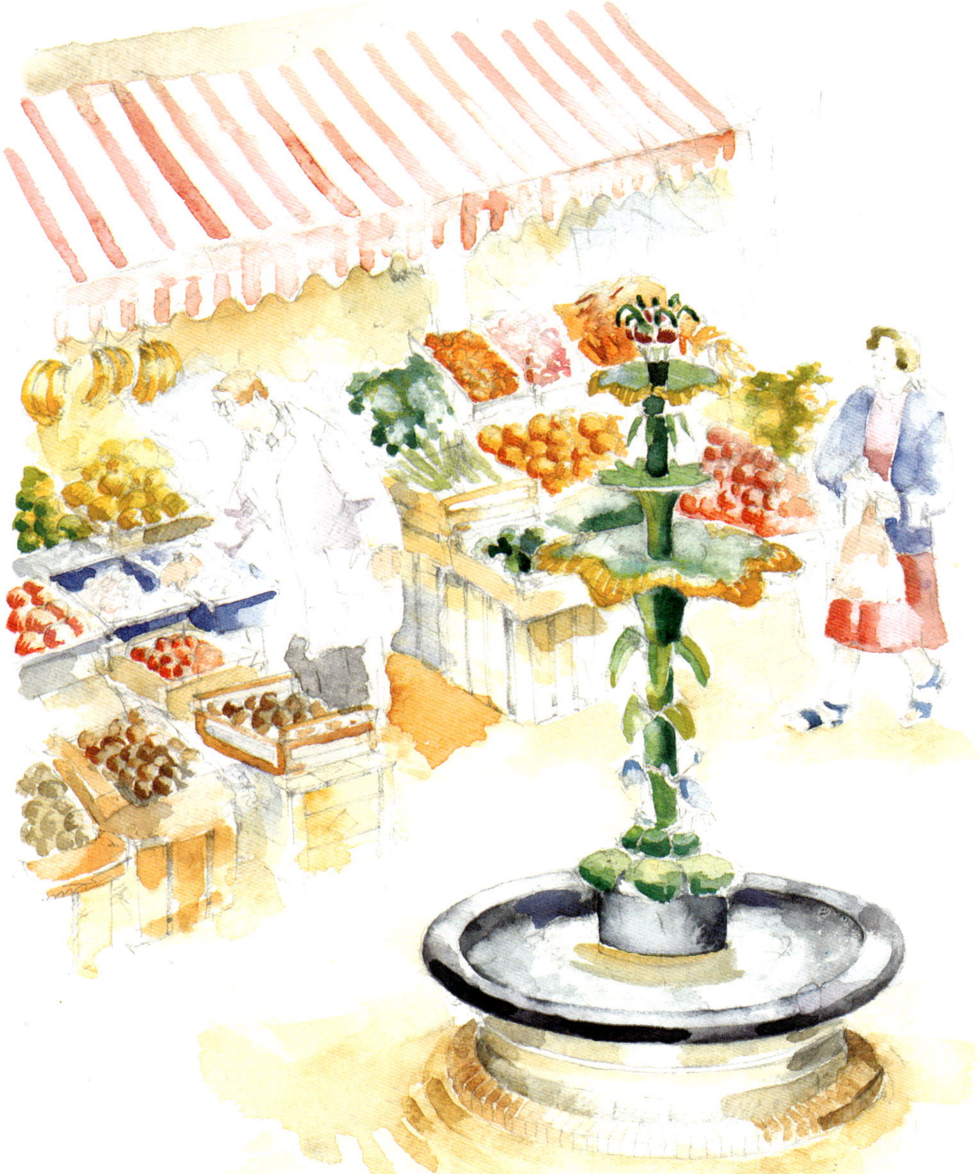

Deireadh Fómhair-Samhain ● Oktober-November ●
Octobre-Novembre

1994 OCTOBER-NOVEMBER

Monday Luan Montag Lundi ● Week 45
Bank & public holiday

31

Tuesday Máirt Dienstag Mardi

1

Wednesday Céadaoin Mittwoch Mercredi

2

Thursday Déardaoin Donnerstag Jeudi

3

Friday Aoine Freitag Vendredi

4

Saturday Satharn Samstag Samedi

5

Sunday Domhnach Sonntag Dimanche

6

ENGLISH MARKET
Cork

The English Market is an indoor market selling meat, fish, poultry, fruit and vegetables. The ornamental fountain that has been retained after recent renovations reminds us of the value of a water supply to a market for both man and beast.

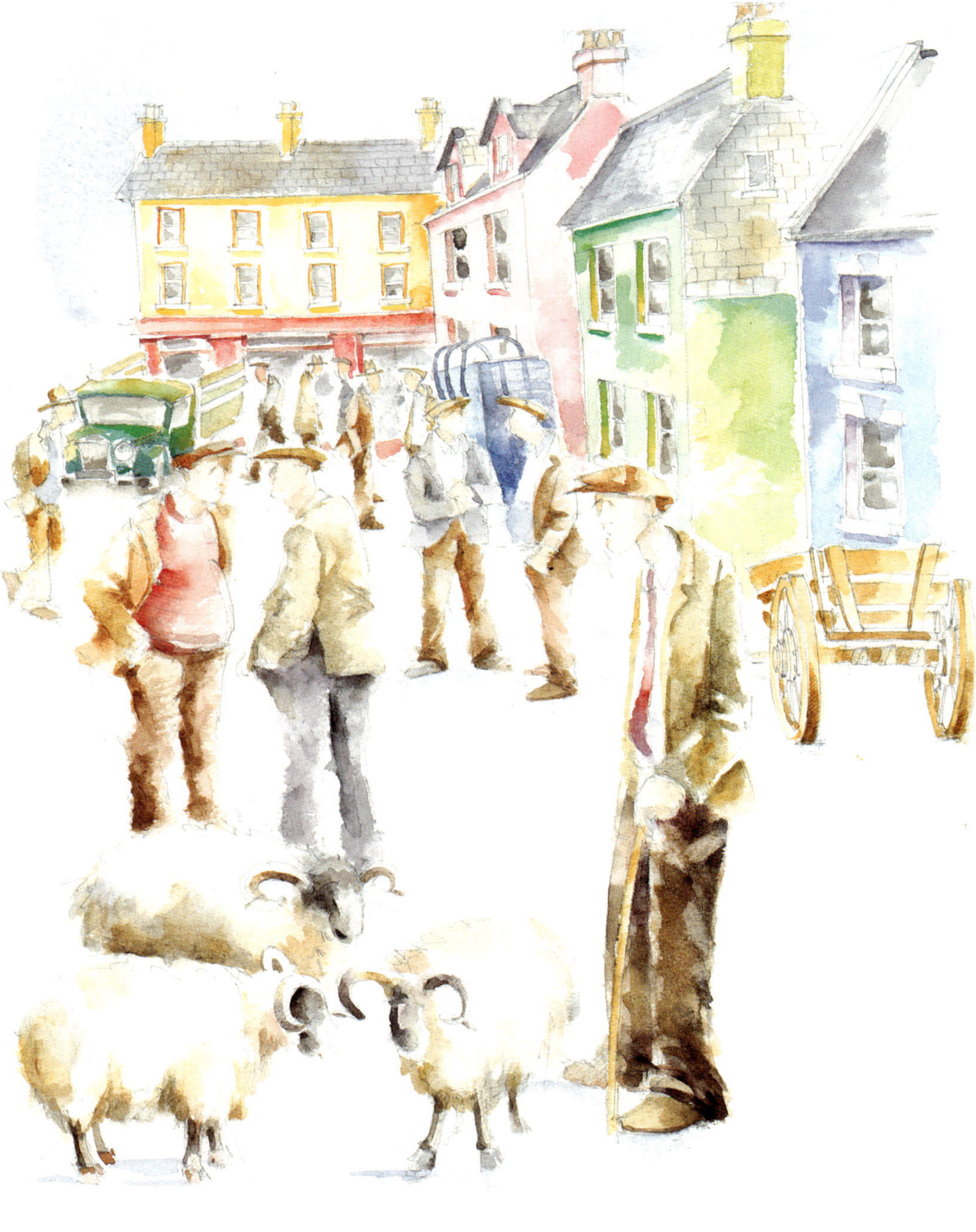

Samhain ● November ● Novembre

1994   NOVEMBER

Monday Luan Montag Lundi ● Week 46   **7**

Tuesday Máirt Dienstag Mardi   **8**

Wednesday Céadaoin Mittwoch Mercredi   **9**

Thursday Déardaoin Donnerstag Jeudi   **10**

Friday Aoine Freitag Vendredi   **11**

Saturday Satharn Samstag Samedi   **12**

Sunday Domhnach Sonntag Dimanche   **13**

FAIR DAY
Dingle, Co. Kerry

Before the Great Famine, Dingle had been a considerable town with a Saturday market serving the densely populated Dingle Peninsula. Its prosperous appearance then was due to a local linen manufacture, an export trade in corn and butter, and the coastal fishery. The population was almost 3,400. Over the next seventy years, however, this figure almost halved, reflecting the loss in County Kerry.

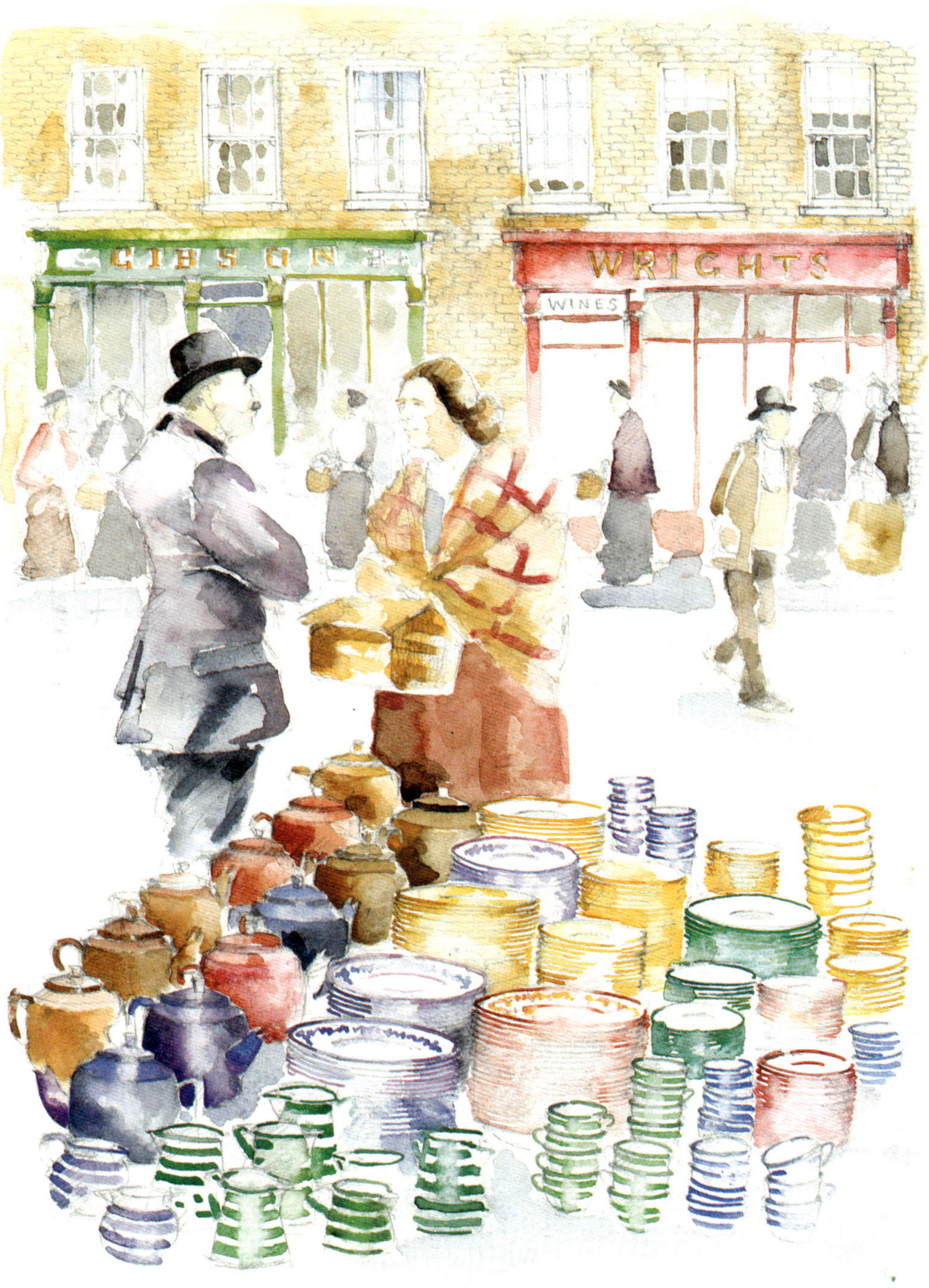
GIBSON 24
WRIGHTS
WINES

1994 Samhain • November • Novembre
NOVEMBER

Monday Luan Montag Lundi • Week 47

14

Tuesday Máirt Dienstag Mardi

15

Wednesday Céadaoin Mittwoch Mercredi

16

Thursday Déardaoin Donnerstag Jeudi

17

Friday Aoine Freitag Vendredi

18

**HIGH STREET
Portadown, Co. Armagh**

Cheap crockery has been imported from Britain since the late eighteenth century and much of it was sold in markets. Pedlars were prepared to exchange it for empty bottles. Dressers in many a home sparkled with the patterned crockery that was the pride of many women. The teapots indicate the Irish weakness for tea.

Saturday Satharn Samstag Samedi

19

Sunday Domhnach Sonntag Dimanche

20

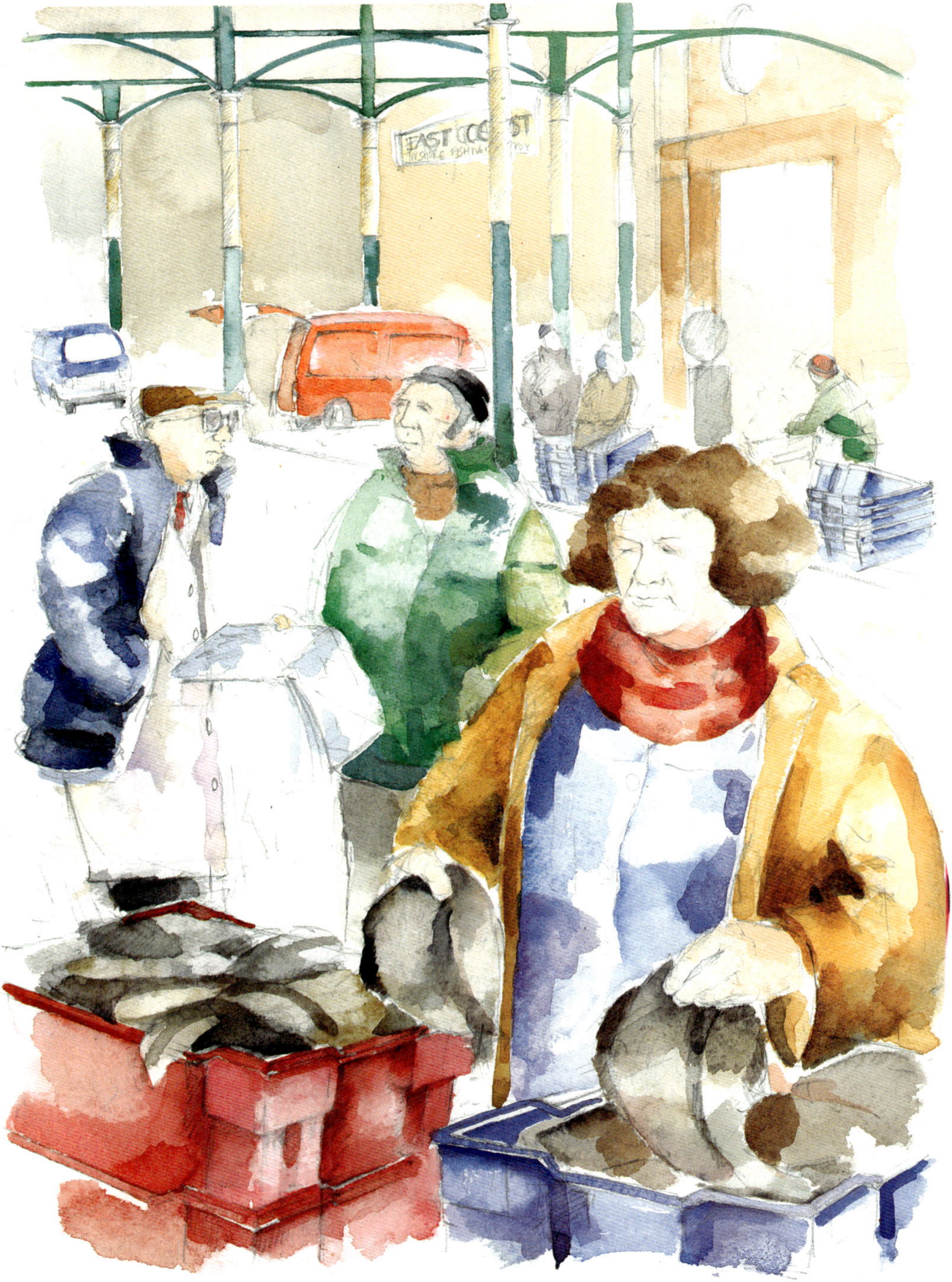
EAST

Samhain • November • Novembre

1994   NOVEMBER

Monday Luan Montag Lundi • Week 48   **21**

Tuesday Máirt Dienstag Mardi   **22**

Wednesday Céadaoin Mittwoch Mercredi   **23**

Thursday Déardaoin Donnerstag Jeudi   **24**

Friday Aoine Freitag Vendredi   **25**

Saturday Satharn Samstag Samedi   **26**

Sunday Domhnach Sonntag Dimanche   **27**

CORPORATION FISH MARKET
Dublin

Dublin was always the major market for the East Coast fishermen. In the early eighteenth century, however, the men from Rush were more likely to be engaged in smuggling tobacco and other contraband from the Isle of Man, and later from France, into Dublin. This traffic was not suppressed until the Coastguard or Preventive Waterguard was established in 1819.

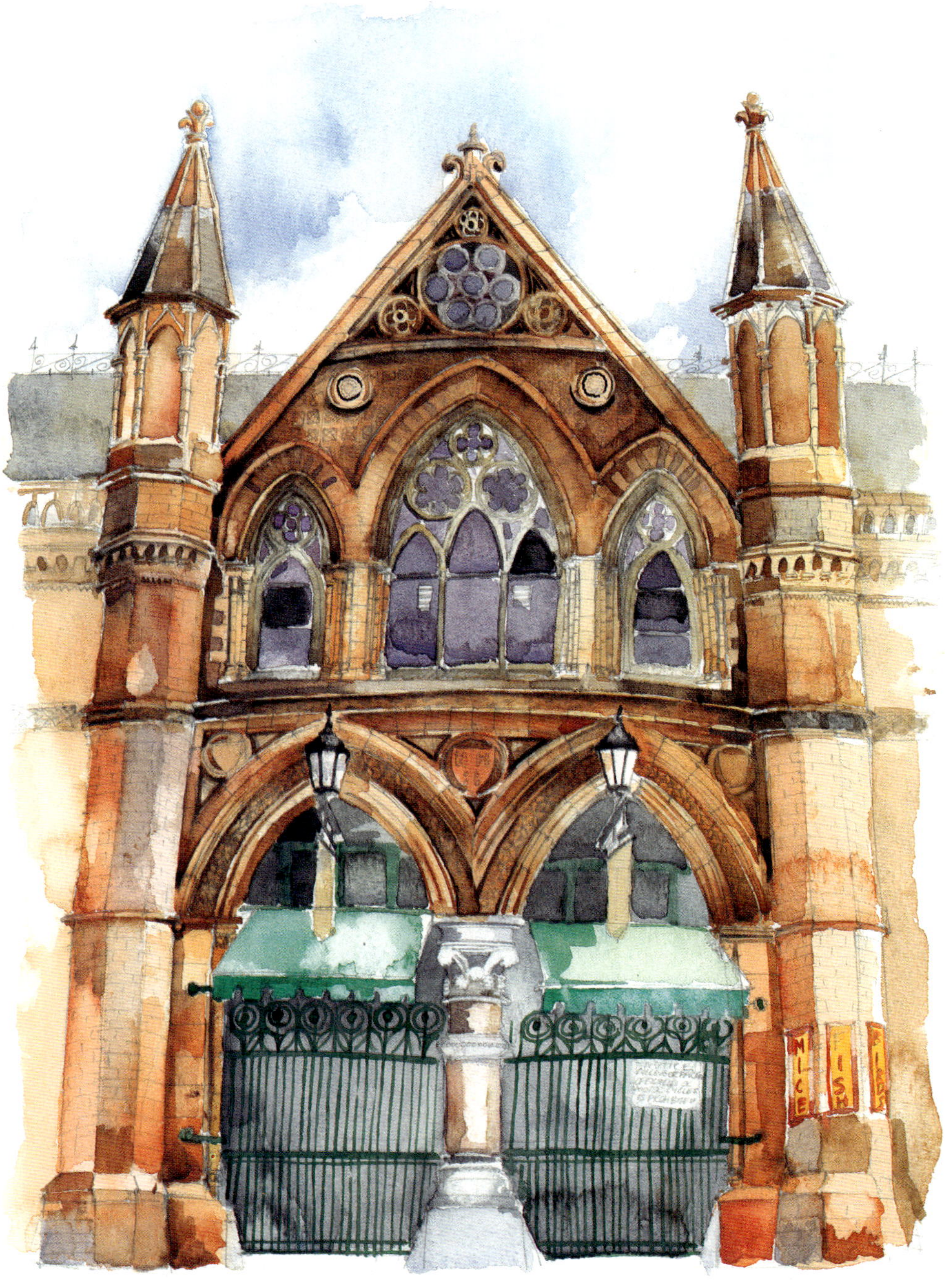
MICE
FISH

Samhain-Mí na Nollag • November-Dezember •
Novembre-Décembre

1994 NOVEMBER-DECEMBER

Monday Luan Montag Lundi • Week 49

28

Tuesday Máirt Dienstag Mardi

29

Wednesday Céadaoin Mittwoch Mercredi

30

Thursday Déardaoin Donnerstag Jeudi

1

Friday Aoine Freitag Vendredi

2

Saturday Satharn Samstag Samedi

3

Sunday Domhnach Sonntag Dimanche

4

SOUTH CITY MARKETS
Dublin

The South City Markets in Dublin's Great George's Street was built in 1881 by a consortium of local businessmen because such retail markets were becoming popular in England. Some critics believed that it could not succeed with the Dublin working classes because it was designed on English lines by an English architect. Nevertheless, when it was accidentally burned to the ground in 1892, the company rebuilt it on a more substantial scale.

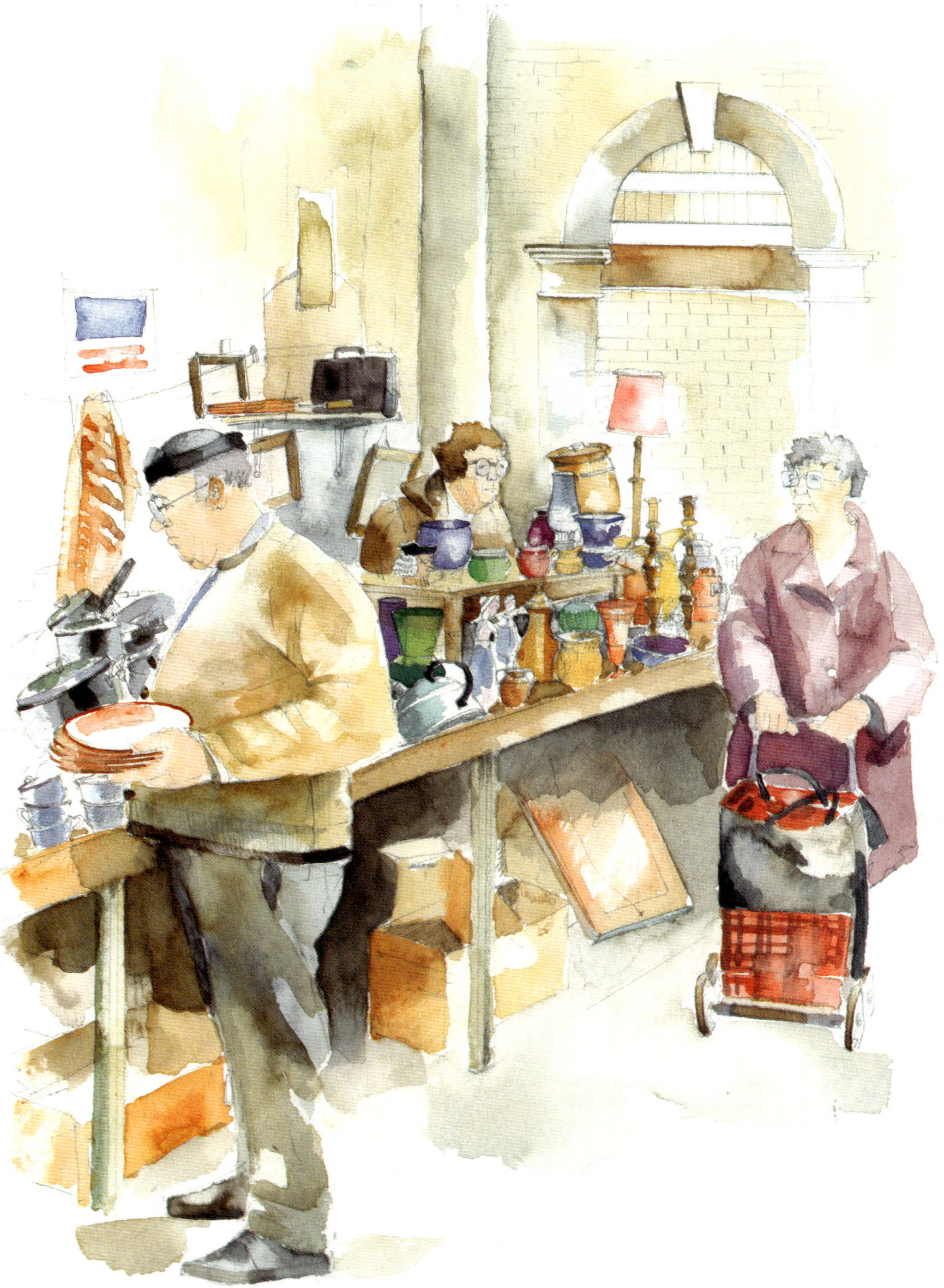

Mí na Nollag • Dezember • Décembre

1994   DECEMBER

Monday Luan Montag Lundi • Week 50   **5**

Tuesday Máirt Dienstag Mardi   **6**

Wednesday Céadaoin Mittwoch Mercredi   **7**

Thursday Déardaoin Donnerstag Jeudi   **8**

Friday Aoine Freitag Vendredi   **9**

Saturday Satharn Samstag Samedi   **10**

Sunday Domhnach Sonntag Dimanche   **11**

ST GEORGE'S MARKET
Belfast

St George's Market is now all that remains of the 41.5 acres of May's Fields that once contained all the major markets of Belfast. When the Fruit and Vegetable Markets were removed a decade ago to the new industrial estate developed alongside the M1 motorway on the Bog Meadows, St George's Market was large enough to contain the remnants.

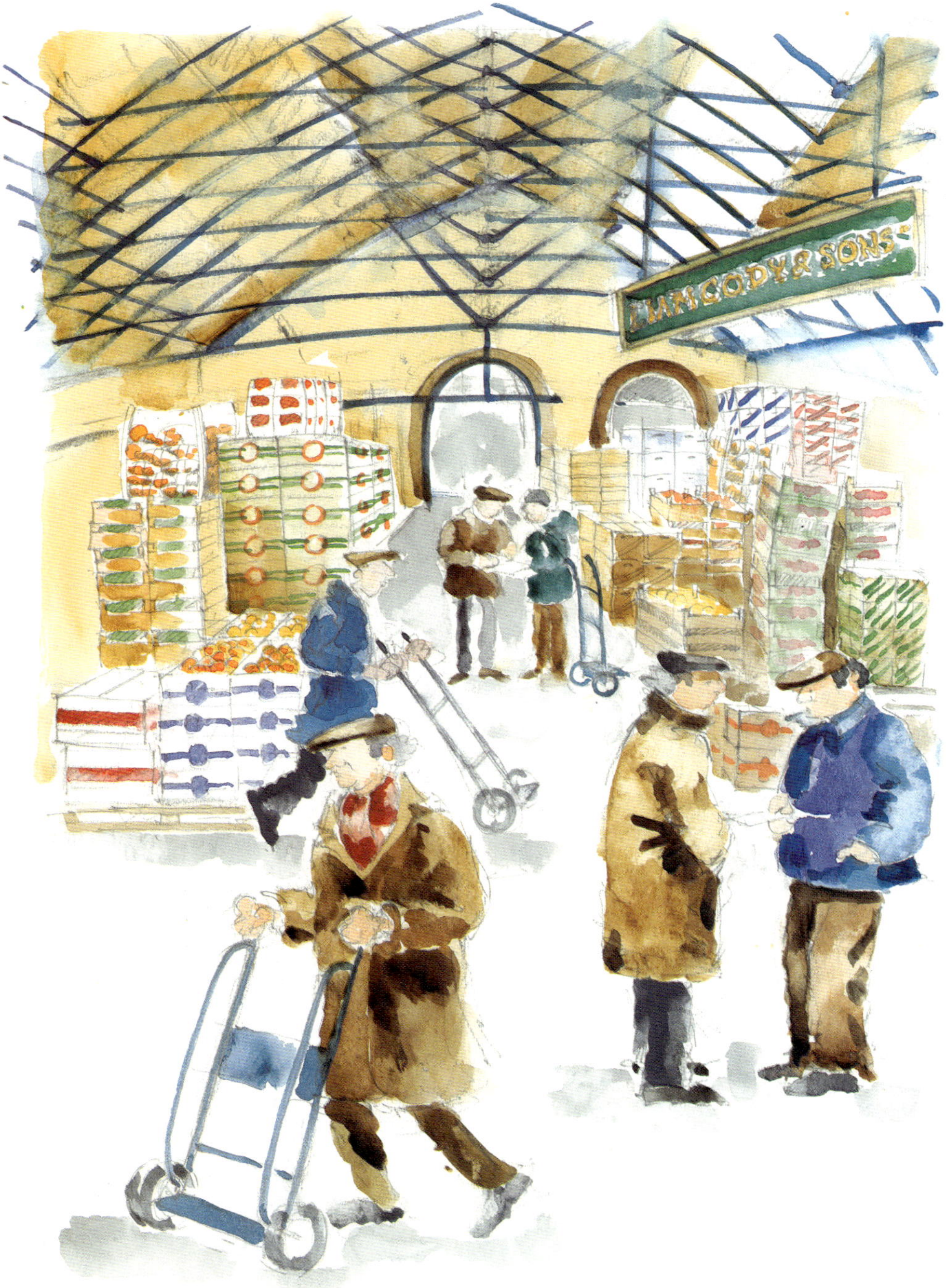
LIAM CODY & SONS

Mí na Nollag • Dezember • Décembre

1994   DECEMBER

Monday Luan Montag Lundi • Week 51   **12**

Tuesday Máirt Dienstag Mardi   **13**

Wednesday Céadaoin Mittwoch Mercredi   **14**

Thursday Déardaoin Donnerstag Jeudi   **15**

Friday Aoine Freitag Vendredi   **16**

Saturday Satharn Samstag Samedi   **17**

Sunday Domhnach Sonntag Dimanche   **18**

CORPORATION FRUIT AND VEGETABLE MARKET
Dublin

The labels on our apples, oranges, bananas and tomatoes make us realise how dependent we have become on foreign countries for fruit and vegetables. New methods of propagation will introduce us to new varieties over the next decade. Our damp and windy climate makes it very difficult for home growers to produce high quality at competitive prices. Market-gardening still has a very important role to play.

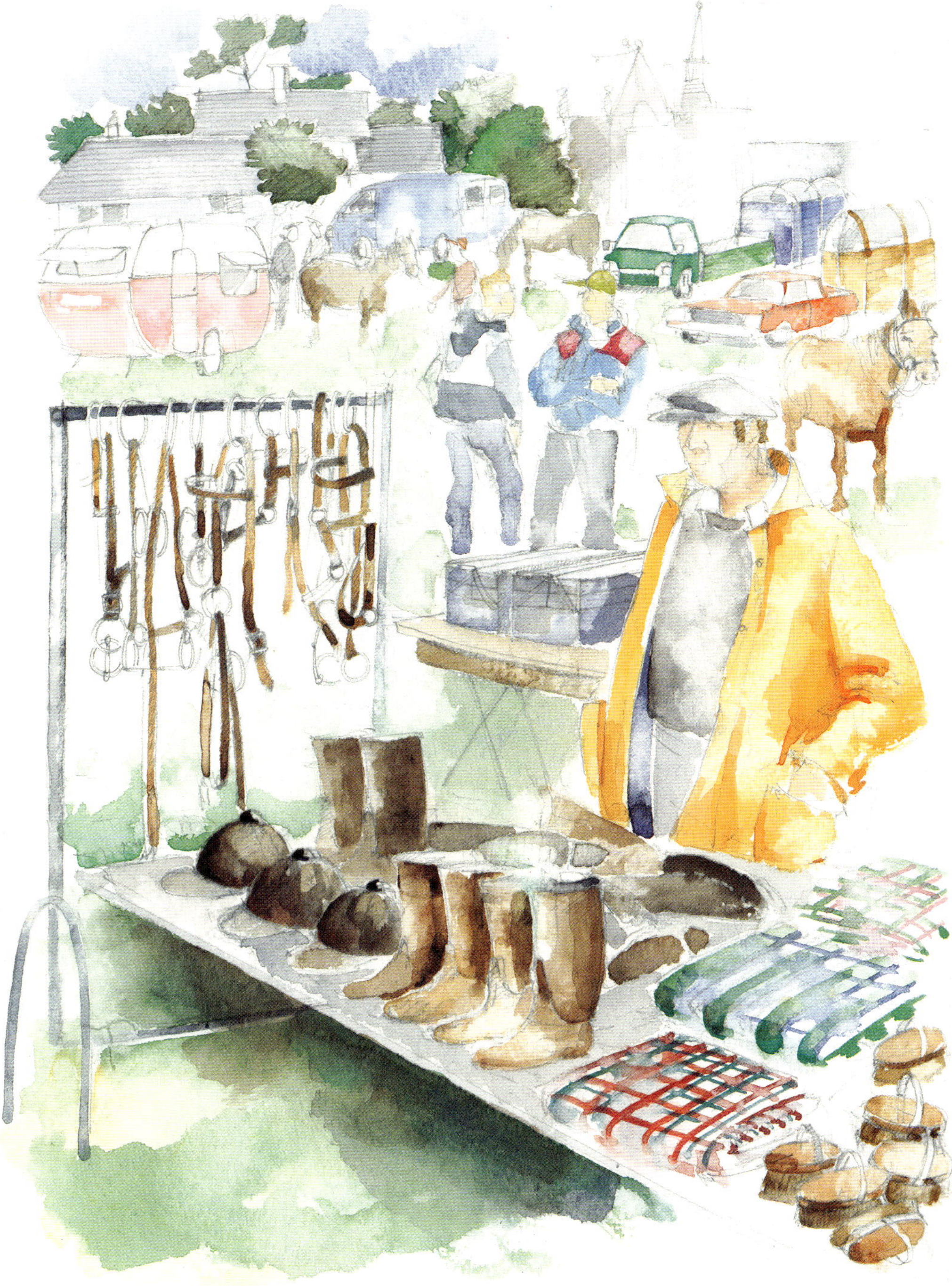

Mí na Nollag • Dezember • Décembre

1994   DECEMBER

Monday Luan Montag Lundi • Week 52

19

Tuesday Máirt Dienstag Mardi

20

Wednesday Céadaoin Mittwoch Mercredi

21

Thursday Déardaoin Donnerstag Jeudi

22

Friday Aoine Freitag Vendredi

23

Saturday Satharn Samstag Samedi
Christmas Eve

24

Sunday Domhnach Sonntag Dimanche
Christmas Day Lá Nollag

25

BALLINASLOE HORSE FAIR
Ballinasloe, Co. Galway

In the traditional fairs hawkers transported and sold all kinds of wares. Charges for tolls and customs in the early nineteenth century included, for instance, 'neck collars or brachims per load'. The hawkers had to follow the fairs because every decent market-town would have had its complement of resident craftsmen.

THE IVEAGH MARKETS MDCCCCVI

Mí na Nollag-Eanáir • Dezember-Januar • Décembre-Janvier

1994-95　　DECEMBER-JANUARY

Monday Luan Montag Lundi • Week 53
St Stephen's Day
Bank & public holiday

26

Tuesday Máirt Dienstag Mardi
Bank & public holiday

27

Wednesday Céadaoin Mittwoch Mercredi

28

Thursday Déardaoin Donnerstag Jeudi

29

Friday Aoine Freitag Vendredi

30

Saturday Satharn Samstag Samedi

31

Sunday Domhnach Sonntag Dimanche
New Year's Day Lá Coille

1

IVEAGH MARKET
Dublin

In 1899 the Iveagh Trust (funded from the profits of Guinness) began to redevelop the district near St Patrick's Cathedral. In 1906 the covered Iveagh Markets were built to take the Patrick Street traders with their second-hand clothes stalls off the streets.

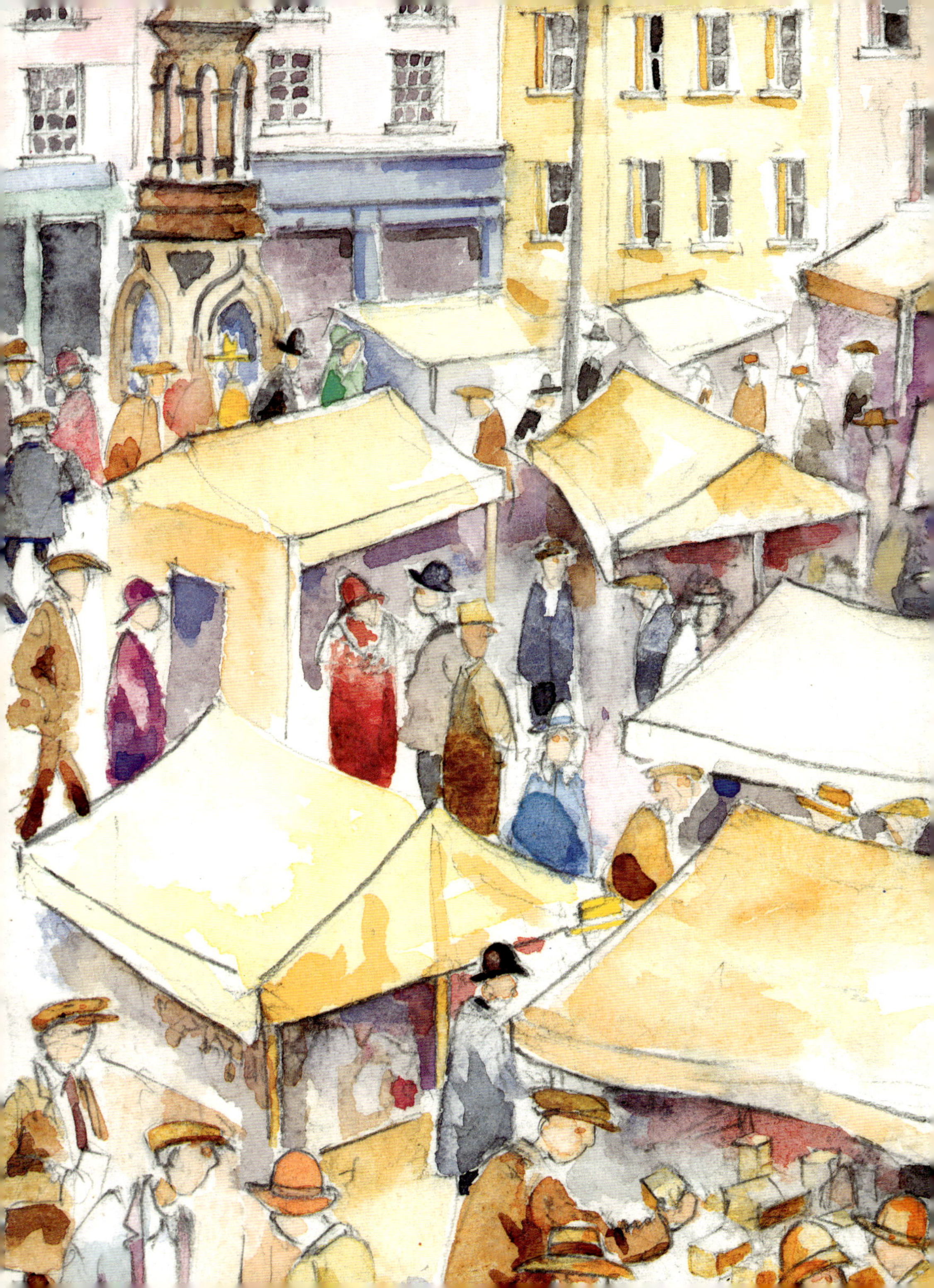